Empath Healing

Survival guide for the highly sensitive person to learn how to become a healer instead of absorbing negative energies from toxic people and connecting to your spirit guides to overcome fears and negative thinking

By Michael Harper

© **Copyright 2020 By Michael Harper - All rights reserved.**

The content contained within this book may not be reproduced, duplicated or transmitted without direct written permission from the author or the publisher.
Under no circumstances will any blame or legal responsibility be held against the publisher, or author, for any damages, reparation, or monetary loss due to the information contained within this book. Either directly or indirectly.

Legal Notice:
This book is copyright protected. This book is only for personal use. You cannot amend, distribute, sell, use, quote or paraphrase any part, or the content within this book, without the consent of the author or publisher.

Disclaimer Notice:
Please note the information contained within this document is for educational and entertainment purposes only. All effort has been executed to present accurate, up to date, and reliable, complete information. No warranties of any kind are declared or implied. Readers acknowledge that the author is not engaging in the rendering of legal, financial, medical or professional advice. The content within this book has been derived from various sources. Please consult a licensed professional before attempting any techniques outlined in this book.
By reading this document, the reader agrees that under no circumstances is the author responsible for any losses, direct or indirect, which are incurred as a result of the use of information contained within this document, including, but not limited to, — errors, omissions, or inaccuracies.

Table of Contents

Introduction 1

Chapter 1.   What is An Empath? 6

Chapter 2.   Characteristic Aspects Of Empathic People? 18

Chapter 3.   Types of Empaths 25

Chapter 4.   The Plight of Empaths 36

Chapter 5.   How to Discover Your Empathy Level 47

Chapter 6.   Healing Through Establishing a Hygienic Routine 61

Chapter 7.   Distinction Between Negative And Positive Empathy .. 72

Chapter 8.   Empaths and Work 84

Chapter 9.   How to Lead a Normal Life as an Empath 93

Chapter 10. Empath Healing Techniques 102

Chapter 11. Empath Self-Care Tips at a Glance 122

Conclusion 138

Introduction

Empathy is the skill to read and know individuals and relate with other people. Occasionally it is charitable and, maybe unprompted, particularly for somebody who was raised with empathy.

People with Empathy are oversensitive persons who undergo extraordinary levels of kindness, understanding, and selflessness. Their powerful empathy generates a fine-tuning fork outcome, where the person appears to experience the sentiments of other individuals. Several people are unconscious of how the infection happens; empaths might have acknowledged for some time that they are insightful to other people. Empaths share numerous personalities with other people.

The sense of passion

Several individuals discover to conceal their genuine sentiments and pretend to the external setting. People with empathy might feel and recount someone's correct feelings is hidden inside rather than what people portray outside. Individuals with empathy undergo compassion towards relatives, children, associates, close friends, aliens, pets, vegetation, and non-living objects. Several are logically more empathic to nature, animals, to the terrestrial classification, motorized instruments, structures, and any diversity of components. Other empaths shall have a blend of various or each of the above-mentioned aspects. Compassion is not restricted to occasion and duration. Consequently, people with empathy might sense the sentiments of other individuals or objects from far.

Understanding yourself is vital

The good logic of understanding involves compassion. Whereas compassion and thought for others are of excellent qualities, they might be challenging for people with empathy.

Occasionally, it might be complicated to differentiate empath feelings from those of other people. This is principally correct when it comes to hurting and pain, which might be challenging both psychologically and physically on somebody who is empathic. Consequently, empaths might become isolated occasionally since the external setting might be a good exhaust on their private power.

On the other hand, there is an unreliable height of power inside people of empathy. The power might be associated with a person's consciousness or their thoughtfulness of the influence of compassion. The consciousness might be influenced by the approval or denial of compassion by people connected to them, comprising relatives of friends. Normally, people with compassionate mature with the affinities; however, they do not discover them for some time. Compassion comprises genetic and religious features. Some researchers assume that compassion is inherited from one age group to another.

How compassion operates

Whereas there is a lot we do not understand how compassion operates, we do have several ideas. Everything has a lively tremor or occurrence and an empath is capable of sensing these feelings. They might distinguish the slightest modifications that are untraceable by a single vision.

Vocabularies of human gestures have vigorous models that begin from the narrator. The gestures have a precise implication to the narrator. In the company of an idiom is an influence known as power. For instance, hatred brings a passionate sentiment that instantly comes with the statement. The term abhorrence becomes reinforced by the narrator's emotions. The individual's sentiments are noticed by people, whether the term is verbal, contemplation, or without oral or non-verbal utterance.

Inability to see suffering or pain

Do you find it difficult to ignore someone who is in pain? Is it challenging for you to turn off your concern for others? If your answer is 'yes' regardless of how busy you are or the challenges you are facing, then it is quite likely that you are an empath. An empath's inability to see pain makes them quite a valuable resource to humankind. For an empath, human life is one of the most valuable resources around and responding to other's needs to come instinctively to them. This is also where the empath's healing ability comes from. Also, this kind of sensitivity makes an empath stand out from the rest.

An empath is attentive, thoughtful, and ensures that others are fine. All these things mean that an empath brings a little happiness to this world. So, if you are an empath, don't hide your gift. Embrace it and welcome it with open arms.

Chapter 1. What is An Empath?

Empathy is the ability to place yourself in someone else's shoes and feel things from their perspective. Healers, nurturers, and highly sensitive individuals who keep on giving of their time, energy, attention, and help, and then continue giving some more, often to the point of exhaustion, are all empaths. An empath is often described as an individual with some paranormal ability to understand the emotional or mental state of those around them.

Empaths are extremely sensitive individuals who are quite aware of the emotions and the energies of others. They tend to assume the emotions of others as their own easily. It can be rather challenging when they don't have any boundaries established and therefore, end up taking on the pain or stress of others. They are quite intuitive and skilled at reading circumstances and people. They are quite perceptive of what meets more than just the eye. Their ability to keenly understand the human psyche makes them natural healers.

Do you ever feel like your heart goes out to somebody regardless of whether they are happy or sad? Can you experience what others feel? Do you feel like you can help those who need a little guidance in life? If yes, then you are probably an empath. The main traits of an empath are as follows.

- Highly sensitive
- Attuned to others' emotions
- Introverted
- Highly intuitive
- Giving
- Easily overwhelmed
- Self-sufficient
- Committed
- Good listener

You will learn more about the traits of an empath in the subsequent sections.

Here are a couple of questions you can ask yourself to determine whether you are an empath are not.

- Do people often refer to you as being emotional or highly sensitive?
- Whenever someone you love feels hurt or overwhelmed, do you feel the same?
- Do you feel physically, mentally, and emotionally drained if you have spent too much time in public?
- Do your feelings get hurt quite easily?

- Do you need some alone time to recharge your batteries after you have been around people for prolonged periods?
- Do you have an unhealthy means of coping with emotional stress like overeating or promiscuity?
- Are you afraid of being in intimate relationships?

If your answer is yes to most or all of the questions mentioned above, then it's quite likely that you are an empath.

Traits Of An Empath

The way an empath sees the world is quite different from the way others see it. An empath is aware of others, their pain, and their emotional needs. Not a lot of people have such a heightened sense of self-awareness. An empath's ability is not just restricted to emotions, but they are also capable of feeling the pain of others around them. Empaths can often sense the emotion or intention of others and understand their perspective too. In this section, you will learn about certain traits of an empath, and if you experience or display these traits, then you will discover that you are an empath too.

Other's emotions

The first sign of being an empath is that you tend to take on the emotions of others as your own. This is a rather classic trait of an empath. Regardless of whether they are displayed or not, an empath can pick up on all these emotions. It is quite likely that you tend to understand what others are feeling even when they don't express themselves tend to experience that emotion as if it was your own. You essentially sponge or absorb the emotions and energies of those around you.

The vibe

Empaths tend to be rather sensitive to the vibe or the feel of their surroundings. They tend to thrive when there is peace and calm around them. This happens because they tend to experience their external environment as internal feelings. Likewise, they can also internalize a chaotic environment.

Understand others

Another core trait of being an empath is that you not only absorb the emotions of others, but you can intuitively sense what someone else is trying to say. Even when others have a hard time expressing themselves, you can easily understand them. On a fundamental level, empathy is all about understanding and connecting with others. So, you tend to understand others' perspectives with ease.

Public spaces

At times, you experience a sudden burst of rather overwhelming emotions whenever you're out in public. You tend to sense the emotions of others, not just while having conversations with them, but also when you are around them. If you are an empath, it is quite likely that you will suddenly experience an emotion that seems to appear out of nowhere or to be precise, from someone else.

Feel physical illnesses

An empath is not only capable of understanding or feeling others' feelings and emotions but can also feel physical illnesses. Whenever you are around someone who is sick or injured, you might even feel that illness as your own. This goes a step beyond feeling sympathy or even some concern toward them. Experiencing the pain they experience, soreness or even tightness in the same areas of the body as theirs is a trait of an empathic brain. Your brain is trying to mirror the feelings and experiences of others. This can be rather uncomfortable. It certainly doesn't sound like something anyone would enjoy. However, this is also one of the reasons why empaths make perfect caregivers. Since they can truly understand what others are experiencing, it becomes easier to care for them.

Influence of television

Even if something horrible or tragic isn't happening to you directly, you can still feel it and experiences as if it were. You might even be able to live through the pain of a tragic event even if it is happening hundreds of miles away from you. You can feel this even if it is a documentary on television. An empath might have a rather strong reaction to violence or tragedy than others and can be easily influenced by any tragic or negative events. So, watching anything that has violence or tragedy embedded in it is not a good idea for empaths.

Advice or opinion

An empath is naturally intuitive. They are also good listeners and tend to wait patiently before offering any advice. They're often insightful as well. A combination of all these traits makes others seek their advice. If you constantly notice that your friends, loved ones, spouse, colleagues or anyone other people in your life come to you when they need advice or opinion on the matter, it might be because of your empathic brain.

Your love

The ability to love comes naturally to an empath. Everyone loves and adores puppies, babies, and even animals. Well, when it comes to an empath, they love with intensity and feel this emotion among many others very intensely. Most empaths simply cannot resist the urge to help a sick puppy or go greet a cat they meet on the street. Whenever you see someone else's child, you tend to experience a strong desire to go over and greet the child. Some people might think that your reaction is a little over the top or even exaggerated. Well, that's the thing about being an empath. Every emotion that you experience tends to get magnified regardless of whether it is good or bad. So, every little positive thing, will tend to make you extremely happy.

Lie detector

There might have been times in the past when someone has deceived you. Well, in hindsight, you might have realized that you were going against your gut instinct. Since empaths are quite intuitive and insightful about the feelings of others, they are like walking lie detectors. You often tend to realize what others are feeling even when they haven't expressed it themselves. The empath's ability to process the minute social cues makes it quite difficult for others to hide their true intentions. Even if you are not precisely aware of what the other person wants, you can determine whether they are honest or not. So, in the future, if you feel like someone is acting a bit strange or isn't being truthful, then trust your gut.

Overwhelmed by intimacy

Relationships are never easy, and they're especially challenging for an empath. If you can sense every irritation, lie or negative emotion that your partner is experiencing, it can take a toll on your mood too. Not just the negative emotions, but even the positive ones can be quite overwhelming favor. At times, you might even feel like you're being engulfed by the relationship. Does this sound familiar to you?

Not just this, but even sharing your space or environment with someone else can hinder your energy. When you are cohabiting with someone else, their energy will always be a part of your energy. Most empaths tend to think of their home as their sanctuary or haven where they can get away from others. Well, if you throw a partner into this mix, it does become difficult to balance your energy. There are ways in which you can cope in a relationship, but the intimacy of a relationship can be overwhelming for an empath. If you can get your private space or find a partner who understands and respects your boundaries, it will become easier to be in a relationship.

A calming effect

As much as people tend to turn to empaths for advice, they also find solace in their presence. Therefore, it is quite obvious that people tend to seek out the most empathic friends whenever they face challenging circumstances. If you work on it, then you can develop this skill too. You can help others process their emotional baggage and help heal them. If you don't acknowledge your empathic abilities or keep hiding your sensitivity, then you won't be able to do any of this. So, as an empath, the first thing you must do is embrace yourself and your gift.

Difference Between Empath And Highly Sensitive People

Did you know that there is a difference between an empath and a highly sensitive individual? Most people tend to use these words synonymously, but they are not the same. A highly sensitive person or HSP tends to have a very sensitive nervous system and is aware of all the subtleties in his surroundings. He or she can be easily overwhelmed when placed in a stimulating environment. All empaths are extremely sensitive to energy; the difference between the two lies in the ability to perceive and feel the feelings of others. An empath can feel and experience the emotional, mental or even the physical state of the other person. This ability must not be confused with empathy.

All humans have empathy, except sociopaths who are incapable of understanding others' emotions. For instance, if a colleague loses his partner, most humans can empathize with him and the tragedy he faced. Others might not fully feel what he is feeling, but they tend to understand his loss. An empath might experience what that person is going through. An empath not only senses others' grief but also experiences the physical, mental or emotional state of the other person. An empath's mind can successfully mimic anxiety, stress, grief, and hurt that the other person feels. An empath will also experience the loss that his colleague has sustained. If your friend has a headache and you are an empath, then you might also feel that headache your friend has. Do you understand this difference here?

A highly sensitive person (HSP) might be easily overwhelmed by the idea of losing their partner because of their sensitive nervous system. It is quite likely that an HSP might even take his colleague's tragedy and make it all about himself. An HSP can quickly go on a downward spiral and start thinking that this world is too bleak and that no good exists. At this point, an HSP is not trying to put himself in the shoes of his colleague but is trying to use his colleague's pain as an excuse for the pain he feels.

This doesn't mean that all highly sensitive people tend to misappropriate emotions, but a lot of them do. An HSP can be triggered by the energy present in his surroundings. Once it triggers a reaction in them, from that point on, it only becomes about themselves and not others around them. HSPs cannot have a direct experience of what the others are feeling whereas an empath can. That said, both HSPs, and empaths, find it rather tricky to deal with emotions. A highly sensitive nature doesn't make everyone a healer.

An HSP is quite reactive to energy, and they usually project their energy or sensitivity onto others. They tend to assume that others are feeling what the HSP is projecting by himself. Since an HSP is often consumed by their emotional state, it is quite likely that they don't understand what the other is feeling. An HSP might not even realize that they have shifted the focus onto himself and will use others and their emotions to validate his reality. They are so absorbed with their reaction that they cannot notice if the subject in question has changed.

HSP tend to have a hard time deciphering the emotions or feelings of others. They are certainly good at picking up on any minute changes in energy around them, but they have also pieced together a story in their head about why someone else's acts the way they do. Since they can be sensitive and quite reactive, they tend to make assumptions about others. The HSP is merely projecting his emotions and feelings onto others. While doing so, the HSP also believes that the other is experiencing what he is projecting.

Since empaths experience and feel what others do, they tend to have a hard time discerning what they truly feel. All empaths are highly sensitive. So, there might be times when their reactive tendencies like projecting emotions come to the forefront. Usually, empaths tend to draw out the emotions of others instead of projecting them. An empath might find it quite difficult to deal with a highly sensitive person. That being said, they could also be quite compassionate and kind. The difference between an empath and HSP is that the latter's emotional stance is usually in a self-protective mode. So, if the person that they're trying to help says or does something which triggers the HSP, then their empathy vanishes and instead, their emotional wounds take precedence.

All empaths can be HSPs, whereas all HSPs don't have to be empaths. The main difference between the two lies in the way they process energy. An empath can literally feel what the other person is feeling, whereas an HSP is merely perceptive of the changes in energy around.

Chapter 2. Characteristic Aspects Of Empathic People?

As an Empath you get an understanding rather well of certain things that have a strong influence on your being. Whether it is your emotional state, your health, your physical wellbeing, or your overall energy levels, Empaths are sensitive to a variety of things, people and places that can have a negative impact on their health and happiness.

As you become more familiar with your role as an Empath, consider some of the following possibilities:

1. Are you sensitive to other people's voices or odors to the point that it is hard for you to be around them?
2. Do bright lights or overcrowded rooms or spaces cause you to feel anxiety or fear?
3. Are you imbalanced around certain people in your home or work life?
4. Do you have a sensitivity to certain foods or beverages, more than other people you know?
5. Do you easily get sick, including allergic reactions, or flu-like symptoms and wonder how you could possibly be that sick all of the time?
6. Do you live with someone who makes you feel uncomfortable whenever you are close to them

physically or emotionally, whether they are a roommate, friend, spouse or child?

7. Have you ever felt the urge to immediately leave a building, house or venue because you didn't like the way it felt inside?

8. Do you have an "allergic reaction" to other people's energy?

9. Have you often found yourself feeling unwell after a party or a group meet up?

10. Are there important moments in your life that you had to cut short or walk away from because of anxiety, panic, of fear?

These questions and many others can help to shed light on exactly WHAT Empaths are sensitive to. It varies from person to person and many Empaths share similar qualities in how they react to certain stimuli in their lives. Here are some examples of what an Empath may be sensitive to on a regular basis:

- Harsh or hateful words
- Attitudes of contempt, rage, anger, jealousy and ego
- Other people's repressed emotions that are projected
- Crowds, whether small or large
- Energy vampires, or someone who drains you of your own energy because of their own emotions, drama, or excessive energy around your empathic energy

- Physical discomfort coming from another person or animal, and sometimes even plant life
- Major changes in environment, or living situation, including career changes, office movement, large moves to new cities and anything involving having to leave a comfort zone
- Travelling, especially in large airports and to large cities
- Foods that are highly processed and generic and have low nutritional value
- Caffeine, sugar, alcohol, drugs
- Medications, especially prescription drugs instead of herbal and natural remedies
- Various forms of energy from emotional states represented through shouting, yelling, crying, laughing, sighing, pacing, sweating, shifting, and fidgeting
- Subways, buses, and all forms of public transportation that involve being in close quarters with many strangers
- Sensitivities that come from allergic reactions to beverages, food or drink that are high in unnatural ingredients or that have been manufactured in industrial machinery

- Many people all at once, even for enjoyment or entertainment, such as in a movie theater, concert, lecture hall, march or parade, ceremony, or event
- Nervous tension, anxiety, or depression, brought on by other people or circumstances
- Hidden emotions that are raw and fresh from other people
- Strong aromas, such as perfume, decay, body odor, breath, unhealthy internal body odors of another (some Empaths can smell cancer or terminal illnesses coming from a person who may or may not be diagnosed)
- Strong feelings on either side of the spectrum, from happy to sad, from one person or a group of people
- Relationship drama from someone else's experience that can be carried into your own
- Other people's deceitfulness or lack of honesty in various situations

The list goes on and it is possible that you have felt some, none, or all of these. You could still be an Empath and have none of these specific sensitivities but may have an awareness of other things, people or places that you are sensitive to. It is important to keep in mind that as you learn more about Empaths, you recognize that it is each person's journey and that no two people are exactly alike. All Empaths have a different experience in uncovering their gift and have to really listen in and develop a strong personal awareness with their own experience.

You may already know that you are an Empath and how you are sensitive to a variety of things and it is always good to remember other ways you can be sensitive. The closer you get to your empathic gift, the more sensitive you can become to receiving and processing the energy that is all around you.

Part of understanding the sensitivities of the Empath is to make sure that you can discover what you are sensitive to so that you can learn how to change that experience. If you are sensitive to strong odors and bright lights, you may try to avoid these kinds of things in your own home, but may have to find ways to accept them or ground yourself well when you go out in public places or spend time in other households.

You may be sensitive to the energy of large groups and find yourself feeling overwhelmed and anxious in those situations, so you may have to enjoy your concert experiences through a television broadcast or from a higher balcony seat where you can have some separation from the main crowd.

You may be sensitive to certain people's energy in your close circle of friends and find it hard to stay in their company for very long because it feels physically and emotionally draining for you to be around them. You might have to limit your friendship with them, or even step away from them all together until you can safely build better boundaries and grounding techniques so that you can spend time in their close company with more internal balance.

Whatever you are sensitive to as an Empath, there is always a solution that can help benefit your journey toward embracing your gift and becoming more empowered as a healing soul. You do not have to live the life of a hermit because of your sensitivities, however it is beneficial to know your sensitivities so that you can provide yourself with the proper tools to maintain a balanced, healthy and happy life as an Empath.

Chapter 3. Types of Empaths

If anyone ever tried to tell you that they knew exactly who you were and what you were like because they knew someone else with the same first name as you and they assumed that all people with that same name are exactly the same, you would probably look at them like they are crazy.

After all, sharing a single name with someone does not mean that you are the same thing.

In the same sense that two people sharing your name are not two iterations of you, yourself, the empath is not a one-size-fits-all sort of label.

No two people are exactly alike.

They may have different likes and dislikes, or preferences in general.

They may want different things out of life to feel fulfilled, or they have different tastes in their relationships.

Just as no two people are alike, no two empaths are alike either.

They actually come in several widely different forms, with different preferences of their own that directly impact their daily lives and the way that they choose to live.

While empaths may exist in several different forms with their own preferences, what is true is that they are all highly sensitive, highly empathetic individuals.

The difference is who they are empathetic towards and how they recharge the best.

Thus far, we have been referring to emotional empaths, who are by far the most common type of empath to encounter.

However, it can be helpful to understand that some people have very different manifestations of their empathic tendencies.

As you read through this chapter, you will be introduced to the six most common types of empaths that exist.

Emotional Empath

The kind of empath that most people think of when they hear the blanket term of "Empath" is the emotional empath.

This individual is the one who is likely to pick up on the emotions of other people.

The emotions of that person standing next to you in line will be picked up, even if you never really interact with the person that is there.

You may never even see the person's face, but you can feel the emotions effectively emanating off of them, and they become your own as well.

Just being around someone in a foul mood can immediately put you into a foul mood as well because you are able to sense and absorb it.

To try to understand this, think about how furniture or clothing simply absorbs the odors in the air around it.

In the same sense, the emotional empath absorbs the emotions that are in the air and reflects them as their own.

Emotional empaths can run into the problem of having too much feedback from all sides, particularly in crowds, which can make them seem shy or introverted—they try to avoid being overwhelmed by the sheer amount of emotions that surround them and that can make them seem like they are uninterested in interactions with other people.

These people must develop the ability to differentiate between what they are feeling as their own emotions and the emotions of other people.

Because they simply absorb the feelings of others, it can be difficult at times to determine whether they are emotional because it is their own true feeling or because it is the feeling of someone around them.

Physical Empath

The physical empath is slightly different—with the physical empath, you are absorbing the energy of the body instead of the heart or mind.

These people are able to be around someone and tell what is physically ailing them.

Think of those who seem to have a knack for always knowing exactly what they have to do to help those around them feel better—they may very well be a physical empath.

The physical empath is able to draw on their own intuition and ability to read other people to instinctively know what the problem is.

They may not be aware of it, but they are able to see the problem and act accordingly.

Even further, however, the physical empath is able to feel the ailment of the other person as well.

They see someone with a cut on their arm, and their own arm hurts; for example—they are able to tell what is wrong, and they are able to sense and feel the pain of the other person as well.

If you happen to be a medical empath, you may unintentionally pick up symptoms from other people.

To better understand this, think of how it seems to be common knowledge that some men, when their partners are pregnant, have their own pregnancy symptoms, despite the fact that there are no changes to the man's body.

The man is able to sort of empathize with the changes to their partner's body, and they feel similar feelings in their own as well in response.

Geomantic Empath

Sometimes referred to as environmental empathy, those who are geomantic empaths feel incredibly in-tune with the world around them.

They find themselves influenced strongly by wherever they are and the health and energy of that site.

They may find that some sites are stressful or negative, or that other sites help them to feel more stable and in control.

Many geomantic empaths do not even realize that they are one in the first place.

The geomantic empath is particularly drawn to certain areas that may be meaningless to others.

This could be a certain landscape or a building of significance.

You may also feel more likely to absorb any energy remaining in a site that has had significant trauma or tragedy, such as feeling energy left behind after someone has died in a home.

You may also feel a close link to the emotion felt by those on that particular land or in that particular building, being able to sense joy or sadness that had once occurred.

Beyond that, however, the geomantic empath is also likely to be highly aware of the world around them.

They feel pain when the trees around them are cut down, or when they see that some landscape has been damaged or defaced.

They want to see the earth maintained and kept healthy, and when it is not, they feel like they owe it to the world to help fix the problem.

If you happen to be a geomantic empath, you are probably drawn to nature—you feel like you want to go out in nature on a regular basis in order to interact with it and recharge yourself.

You find that your own energy is recharged when you spend time in the quiet surroundings of a forest or otherwise on your own in a natural environment.

Because you find peace in nature and harmony, you likely feel the need to bring that back into your own home life as well.

You may have many plants that you care for or choose to have all wood furniture in order to have a piece of nature within your own home.

Plant Empath

The plant empath is, as you may infer, someone who is particularly empathetic toward plants.

If you happen to be a plant empath, you are able to understand and sense what the plants around you need.

Plants are unable to communicate, but you are still able to nurture and care for them in a way that meets and exceeds their needs, so they are able to flourish.

You are probably considered to have some sort of gift when it comes to taking care of plants, such as your friends and family deeming you to have a green thumb, or you may intentionally work in a career line that has you directly interacting with plants on a regular basis.

The plant empath is likely to choose work such as a farmer, maintaining a park, or working as a gardener, and for good reason—they are able to put their skills to the test effectively.

They are able to ensure that the plants are tended to while also feeling like they are recharging themselves as well.

The plant empath feels closely aligned with the plants around him or her, and they feel at ease when surrounded by them, whether in the wilderness or at home in a garden.

If you are a plant empath, you will require constant contact with plants of some sort, and you may even have a special tree that you relate to or like to spend time with, in order to recharge, such as a tree that was planted in memoriam for someone you loved.

Animal Empath

Empaths, in general, tend to feel some sort of connection and understanding for animals as they are able to empathize with living beings.

However, some people feel even more in tune with animals than others, and they are able to sense far more about what their animals want or need.

These people are animal empaths, and they are usually found alongside an animal companion of sorts.

Typically, these animal empaths will dedicate their lives to taking care of animals in some way, whether they have several pets of their own, they run a pet store, work in a shelter, or work in an animal sanctuary or other animal-based lines of work.

They may even be veterinarians or people that go out and volunteer to rehabilitate wild animals that have been injured.

As an animal empath, you may feel the need to spend time with your animal companion in order to recharge and feel energized and rested.

For example, if you have a horse that you take care of regularly, you may find that you only feel rested and recharged after a good horse riding session, and that would be your method of recharging when you felt stressed or overwhelmed about something.

In particular, animal empaths are regularly found studying animals and learning as much as they can about their animal companions.

They may choose to study veterinary medicine or discover how to become an ethical animal trainer.

So long as they are able to live their life with interaction with animals, they are satisfied.

Intuitive Empath

The last form of empath that will be discussed in this chapter is the intuitive empath.

This person is able to pick up information about others just through spending time with them.

They are able to tell what someone is or what kind of person they are just by looking at them and inferring details based on their own intuition.

These people are commonly expected to be psychics or able to read minds when in reality, they are simply really good at picking up on cues intuitively.

These people are closely in tune with the energy around them and are able to put it together effectively in order to figure out what is going on in the minds of others.

If you happen to be an intuitive empath, for example, you may be able to tell just by being around someone that they are a mother or that they are going through a rough time just by spending that time with the other person.

They never had to say a word to you about who they were as an individual or what their experiences were—you simply knew on your own.

When you are an intuitive empath, however, you tend to be even more sensitive to being in large crowds than the emotional empath.

You can quickly and easily get overwhelmed by other people because you are constantly taking in information about those around you.

Chapter 4. The Plight of Empaths

While empathy can offer importance to our lives, it is warned that it can likewise turn out badly if a line isn't drawn. While demonstrating an empathetic reaction to the disaster and misfortune of others can be useful, it can likewise, whenever misled, transform us into emotional parasites.

When empaths lose track of reasonable empathetic response, it can lead to several negative impacts on their lives. It is good to be good, but too good never did well to anyone.

Sympathy can aggravate individuals, so on the off chance that they erroneously see that someone else is compromising an individual they care for. Hostility may arise as one may misinterpret the intentions of others. For instance, if someone is trying to hug your child, an empath (being too sensitive) may wrongly read another person as a threat. Although you are trying to protect your child, your paranoia might turn out into an inconvenience for the person whose intentions were not malicious. Thus, sympathy and hostility are also described as "existential twins."

Not only that, empaths tend to lose money more than usual; sometimes, to the point where they end up penniless. For a considerable length of time, instances of excessively compassionate people imperiling the prosperity of themselves and their families by giving ceaselessly their life investment funds to destitute people have served as the prime example. Such excessively compassionate individuals who feel they are by one way or another in charge of the misery of others have built up empathy-based blame.

The blame goes on to the point of self-ridicule as well. The state of "survivor blame" is a type of sympathy-based blame in which an empathic individual erroneously feels that their very own satisfaction has come at the expense or may have even caused someone else's wretchedness. People who normally carry on of compassion-based blame, or neurotic philanthropy, will, in general, create gentle discouragement in later-life.

Since money is involved, it must be remembered that a lot of us have families who need our care, empathy, and love. The neurotic philanthropy can damage relationships if an intervention is not sought. The main thing which must be remembered is that empathy ought to never be mistaken for affection. Love isn't enough to cement the bonds; stable and better finances play a massive role as well. While love can make any relationship better, empathy can't. Love can fix, compassion can't. One who is getting involved in empathetic spending must carefully weigh their priorities. For instance of how even good-natured empathy can harm a relationship, we must look around ourselves.

Not only do people end up being bankrupt while trying to help others, but the vines of empathy can also wrap onto their physical, mental and emotional states. Empathy fatigue or weariness" alludes to a condition of physical fatigue coming about because of rehashed or delayed individual inclusion in the constant sickness, incapacity, injury, distress, and loss of others. An empath can become so involved in the welfare of others that they may forget their well-being. Any excessively sympathetic individual can encounter compassion exhaustion.

On top of it, if an empath encounters a narcissist, it's done for. So, we need to understand the opposite side as well.

Narcissism

As a matter of first importance, we have to comprehend what are narcissism, abuse, and narcissistic abuse to understand how they can damage empaths.

Narcissistic Personality Disorder alludes to self-important conduct, an absence of compassion for other individuals, and a requirement for the reverence which must all be reliably clear at work and seeing someone. Narcissistic individuals are much of the time depicted as arrogant, conceited, manipulative, and needy. Narcissists may focus on impossible individual results and might be persuaded that they merit exceptional treatment. Narcissism is a variant of Narcissistic Personality Disorder. It includes presumptuousness, manipulative nature, childishness, linear thought processes, and vanity-adoration for mirrors.

Narcissists will, in general, have high confidence. Be that as it may, narcissism isn't simply something very similar regard; individuals who have high confidence are frequently unassuming, though narcissists once in a while are. It was once imagined that narcissists have high confidence superficially, yet where it counts they are uncertain. Nonetheless, the narcissists are secure or self-important at the two levels. Spectators may construe that instability is there because narcissists will, in general, be cautious when their confidence is undermined or they are being criticized; narcissists can be hostile when they feel that they are being attacked. They tend to read between the lines a lot more than necessary. The occasionally hazardous way of life may all the more by and large reflect sensation-chasing or impulsivity such as reckless spending. Narcissists don't need empathy in the manner we commonly accept – they need empathy, regret, and lament-- all of which they lack.

We learned that a lot of us equate feelings like sympathy with empathy; however as referenced over, an individual can comprehend what someone else feels, thinks, and encounters without inclination the human feelings that accompany it. Narcissists lack it. So, it will, in general, let them free for harmful conduct. The narcissist's absence of compassion thought infers that their oppressive conduct is unexpected. It's amazingly manipulative and very purposeful when they are dealing with people who are highly receptive of them, especially the empaths.

Empaths Facing Narcissist Abuse

Individuals who are shafts separated may be drawn together for all inappropriate reasons. The pairing of an empath and a narcissist is a 'poisonous' fascination bound for disaster.

Most of the times, empaths embrace people's emotions and needs as they have been in a condition, in childhood or somewhere when they were growing up. There are a good number of chances that empaths are the way they are as they have been in a condition of vulnerability or tragedy, and as a result, they have experienced such a great amount of pain that they basically surrender their self-sufficiency, go beyond their financial and emotional means to help others, and do not take a stand for themselves even at the cost of emotional harm. Also called "learned helplessness," it can prompt gloom and other psychological maladjustments. And it is the most lucrative playground for narcissists. Narcissists, for instance, are pulled in to individuals they will get the best use from. Frequently, this implies they seek after and target empaths.

If a narcissist needs to constrain their subject into learned helplessness, the initial step is to set up an association. And empaths, being compassionate, almost always are willing to lend an ear for the distressed person, who could or could not be narcissistic. Intellectual sympathy is a narcissist's weapon for setting up the association.

As should be obvious, the narcissist's absence of empathy is a fantasy since they have to utilize psychological compassion to get what they need from everyone around them. They utilize Emotional Empathy to get what they want, and they do not care about the effect on other people. When someone is desperate for support or assistance or in serious circumstances, they utilize psychological sympathy to get into the subject's head. They have to comprehend the subject's sentiments and thoughts which they would then be able to control into creating a result that is most useful to them. Convenient, isn't it?

That is the reason you've likely wound up bobbing forward and backward commonly pondering about what they feel for you. Narcissists keep empaths on edge. It is much simpler to accept this isn't deliberate. However, these activities are determined. Narcissists decipher feelings like love, receptiveness, thoughtfulness, and liberality as shortcomings. Also, on the off chance that you offer a bit of leeway, they'll take a mile, back up, and travel a similar mile again and again until you're hauling your hair out.

What narcissists see in empaths is a giving, cherishing individual who is going to be dedicated, adoring and most genuine shoulder to lean upon. The very fact that an empathetic person is willing to hear them out makes them alert and interested. Be that as it may, sadly empaths are pulled in to narcissists because from the outset this is about a bogus self. Narcissists present a bogus self, where they can appear to be enchanting and shrewd, and notwithstanding giving until you don't do things their way, and after that they get cold, retaining and rebuffing."

Empaths are something contrary to narcissists. While individuals with narcissistic character issue have no compassion and flourish with the requirement for profound respect, empaths are exceptionally touchy and tuned in to other individuals' feelings. In a way, empaths are like sponges that absorb sentiments from other individuals in all respects effectively. This makes them appealing to narcissists since they see somebody who will satisfy their every need in a benevolent manner.

At the point when a narcissist is attempting to snare somebody in, they will love and mindful, yet their veil soon begins to slip. Toward the starting, they just observe the great characteristics and accept the friendship that will make them look great. This doesn't last since narcissists tend to be loaded with hatred, and they consider most to be as beneath them. When they begin to see their accomplice's faults, they never again deal nicely with them, and soon begin to reprimand them for not being impeccable.

It can at times take some time for the real nature to appear. In any case, this conflicts with an empath's responses, as they believe they can fix individuals and mend anything with empathy. They truly have faith that they can listen more and give more. That is not the situation with a narcissist. And the empaths have a hard time facing that other person is devoid of compassion. It's unbelievable for some empaths that someone simply doesn't have compassion, and that they can't mend the other individual with their affection.

Empaths buckle down for concordance, though narcissists are hoping to do the inverse. They appreciate disorder and like to realize they can pull an individual's strings. This is a strategy narcissists use to reel their accomplice back in. With empaths, it is exceptionally powerful; because they need to help their accomplice and help them develop. Eventually, they are simply being abused further.

Narcissists' strategies on empaths

Narcissists control empaths by leading them on with irregular expectations. They will incorporate compliments and thoughtfulness into their conduct, causing the empathetic individual to accept that if they carry on in the right way, they will recover the happiness of others. And that is what empaths believe in doing. Sad, but a dangerous combination.

The push and pull nature of the narcissistic relationship can create a damaging partnership between the person in question and the abuser, where it can feel practically difficult to leave the relationship, regardless of how much harm it is doing.

With compassion comes the capacity and readiness to take a gander at ourselves and take a gander at our deficiencies and that gets exploited while the toxic bond is going on. It turns into a cycle for an empath who has been immune to self-damage because they begin taking a gander at themselves, and what do they have to do to change, and what do they have to do must be beneficial to others. It's the ideal set up, lamentably.

Evading the cycle of abuse

Besides, the cycle continues until the Empath lose the sense of who they are any more, and feels incredibly exhausted, self-ridiculing and disheartened from endeavoring and missing the mark with the Narcissist over and over. They feel exhausted and disheartened while continuing to evade and redirect their feelings towards themselves to keep up the bond and benefit others. The precise inverse thing they have to do is hurt their tricky Narcissist, who will quickly use the empath's outward renunciation of anger to demonstrate how hurt they have been by them, and as evidence for them being the veritable Narcissist.

The key to an Empath truly vanquishing this cycle and being adequately ready to leave, and retouch, is to truly re-perceive themselves with and feel their annoyance, and recognize that they in conviction cause hurt, and are in like manner allowed to feel rage, and lose their patience and care. That, without a doubt, it is okay to use unskillful or inadequate strategies in characterizing a resentment awakened point of confinement. It is acceptable to anger the narcissist if the latter is to make certain authoritatively going to have their feelings hurt anyway.

That every so often it is critical to use ill will and capacity to get someone to finally back off, in case they have felt equipped for your essentialness, time, and resources, and this doesn't make someone Narcissistic, problematic, or entitled, yet rather is verification of confidence and regard.

Chapter 5. How to Discover Your Empathy Level

The world is short of empathic people, and it needs more of them in every profession for a better world. If you want to know the level of empathy that you have, it can be assessed using Empathy Quotient. Now, let's get down to our determiner.

Are You a Good Listener?

Listening to other people is important in showing empathy. Empathic people listen with their heads and heart. They pay attention to what the other person is telling them without thinking of anything else or fiddling with their phones. They look at the other person in the eye and follow the conversations with a nod here and there as well as acknowledgment comments. So, do you listen to other people's problems without feeling the pressure to fix the problem ASAP?

Are You Emotionally Open?

Now, when we say empathic people are good listeners, it does not mean that the conversation should be one-sided. They should also open up emotionally to build a bridge that will connect you with the other person. Opening up emotionally to someone else is not an easy thing to do, but it is important. Empathic people open up about past situations that are similar to the one at hand to familiarize themselves with the other person's conversation. It makes the other person feel comfortable pouring their heart out to you. Do you find yourself opening up to people to make them feel better and comfortable?

Do You Find Yourself Offering Physical Affection to Vulnerable People?

Empathic people always feel this need to hug someone they feel is vulnerable. It might not be a good move, as some people may not feel okay receiving physical affection. When you hug a person or give them any other physical affection, this act boosts oxytocin levels, which makes the two parties feel better.

Do You Have the Capability to Withhold Judgment?

It is hard to withhold, especially on the first encounter with a person. Empathic people never judge a person when they interact with them for the first time. They take time to have a deep understanding of the other person's perspective before they conclude if it is good or bad. What is your first thought of a person when you interact with them for the first time?

Do You Have Readily Available Help?

Empathic people see the problems people are going through and feel the need to help. They always want to make life easier for other people and expect nothing in return. When we talk of help, it can be something simple as helping an elderly to cross the road, helping your aged aunt locate her glasses. Sometimes you can extend an empathic gesture by just offering help when you see an opportunity to help.

Do Strangers Stir Curiosity in You?

Most people are cautious about strangers, but empathic people are interested in people they know nothing about. Their communication with strangers does not stop on the weather, but they go beyond that and strike a conversation to understand the other person's world. They also open up about themselves to make the other person comfortable. How many times have you ever approached a stranger, especially one you would not talk to in normal circumstances?

Are You Mindful of Your Surroundings?

Empathic people can notice every action, expression, and feelings of the people surrounding them. They notice the sights, smells, and sounds and register them consciously. People walk past things and places and only register them unconsciously. I know you have passed through many places, and most of the time, you cannot remember what you passed along the way. Well, how did you answer the above questions? If you answered yes to six or seven of them, your empathy is extremely high. If your answer was on the affirmative to four or five questions, your empathy is high; two or three questions your empathy is moderate, and if you answered yes to one or none of the questions above, your empathy is low, and you should find a way to develop it.

Signs That Your Empathy Levels Are High

Other than taking the test above, it is possible to know whether you are an empathic person through some traits in a person. Let us look at signs that portray that a person is highly empathic.

- Knowledgeable

Highly empathic people notice and feel things before you tell them. It is not intuition; they know what is happening to the other person exactly, and the more familiar they are to a person the easier it is to know how they are feeling.

- Assuming Ailments and Feelings

Highly empathic people absorb the feelings of other people regardless of the distance. They experience the feelings and experience the symptoms of the other person's ailment, such as body aches, colds, digestive disorders, or lower-back problems.

- Feeling Overwhelmed

They internalize other people's feelings, whether they are indoors or outside. When they are in public places, they absorb the feelings of so many people, and it can be overwhelming.

- They Detest Violence

They are affected by violence in the script or movies. Such kind of violence is unbearable to them, and the more they read or watch, the more they become affected until they have to stop reading and watching altogether.

- They Easily Detect Dishonesty

Highly empathic people will always tell when a person is lying. They will know when a person is lying through their teeth or omitting some truth.

- Addictions

They are prone to addictions from drugs, sex, alcohol to all types of addictions. They turn to addictions to try and protect themselves from the pain they experience when they absorb other people's emotions.

- They Love Nature and Being Alone.

Highly empathic people love the outdoors just to observe and feel the nature. They feel comfortable when they are away from other people, and most prefer the company of animals than people.

- You Can Easily Distract Them.

People with high empathic quotient are easily distracted if they lack enough motivation from school, work, or home. They prefer to do interesting things, and when things are 'boring,' they easily switch off.

- Seekers of Knowledge

Highly empathic people are always seeking information, and they never leave questions answered. When they seek more knowledge, they may develop an overload of information.

- Listeners

People with high levels of empathy are great listeners. They are the people we call when we need a word of advice or simply someone to hear us out. People feel comfortable confiding in them because they know that they care for them genuinely.

- They Cannot Tolerate Egos

Highly empathic people dislike the company of egoistic people. They become drained when they are around such selfish people.

- Mood Swings

They are mostly shy, moody, or aloof because they have absorbed a lot of negative emotions from other people. When they have absorbed too much negative energy from others, they tend to stay away from people and may become unsociable.

- Occupational Difficulties

Highly empathic people are not good at pretending. If they are sad, they will not act happy and vice versa. When they are in a sad state, it burdens them emotionally, and this may cause problems for them in school and at work.

- Residual Energy

Empathic people find a hard time accepting things with previous owners; they have difficulties with antiques, used cars, or old houses.

How to Cope with High Empathy Levels

Empathy is important in our lives for better co-existence. People with high empathy levels should learn how to cope and manage them to avoid being overburdened by their feelings and other people's feelings that they absorb. Most of them try to seek comfort in food and all kinds of addiction.

1. Practice Awareness

Becoming aware of your body is important. Become aware of your feelings as they respond to internal shifts such as mood change, absorbing another person's strong emotions or hormonal change. If you are not aware of your feelings, you will most likely react in a way that will leave you feeling uncomfortable. When you are aware, you consciously choose how to respond, and you choose an action that will not leave you feeling uncomfortable.

2. Understand the Cycle of Energy

A big step to coping with high levels of empathy is to understand that the response you give the environment also gives more strength to the energy. If someone offends you say makes a bad comment about your dressing, and you reiterate by making a worse one on her hair, you only worsen the problem. You will not only hurt the other party, but you will also increase your suffering. You will suffer from the initial hurt caused to you by the other party, and you will also suffer when the other party is suffering because of your hurtful words towards them. If you can train yourself to offer love, instead, you will make the other person, and at the same time, you will experience healing. When you understand that our soul only seeks love, you will put yourself in a position to manage everything else. You should always stick to a place of kindness, love, wholeness, and forgiveness to avoid expressing bad energy in the form of fear, anger, or complaining.

3. Don't Take Things Personally

Highly empathic people suffer because they take other people's problems as their own and feel the same pain as people with suffering. When you realize that nothing is as what you think it is, you will reduce your suffering. Highly empathic people should learn that other people should learn life lessons through the challenges of life. They should realize that everyone has the same power to move past challenges in life as they do. They should allow their loved ones to come out of their cocoon and not try to pull them out. They should also realize that they are not responsible for fixing any situation; their responsibility is on how to manage their energy. Their focus should be on adding goodness, warmth, and love to the people around them.

4. Balance Yourself

The key thing empathic people should always remember to balance themselves is to stay connected to their hearts, and when they find themselves disconnecting because of their thoughts or negative energy from other people, they should know their way back. They can do that through meditating to balance their health, addictions, relationships, or weight. They can as well take a few deep breaths to balance themselves. Highly empathic people should also know that they cannot change who they are, but they can become aware of how they are affected. When they balance with themselves, they realize that they can change how they react and behave regardless of the burden of their emotions and those of others. Did you know that 90% of humans' behavior is from habits? Highly empathic people should learn that they do things because they have done them before, and they are always doing them. They should re-train their brain reacts differently to the same stimuli. When you are highly empathetic, you should know that you have three choices when reacting to negative energy; you can react with negativity, withdraw, or give love.

Signs That You are Not Empathetic Enough

• Involved in Lots of Argument

When you are not empathetic enough, you always find yourself arguing with others a lot. You are always in disputes with family, friends, strangers, and co-workers. When you are not empathetic, you have a hard time understanding the emotions of other people.

- You Think That Other People Are Over-Sensitive

Such a person may crack inappropriate jokes at inappropriate times, and when people react negatively, he or she feels that they are over-sensitive. A person with low empathy quotient has trouble understanding other people's emotions.

- You Don't Think Others Point of View Is Important

Lowly empathic people feel the need to defend their opinions with all vigor and at the same time, do not let others share their opinion. They are excessively critical and cynical.

- Blaming Others

People with low emotional quotient never take responsibility for their mistakes. They always blame others for their direct mistakes and indirect ones. They are always bitter and feel victimized. They have no insight into how their feelings can cause problems.

- They Cannot Comprehend Strong Emotions

They have a problem with coping with emotional situations. They stay away from such situations to hide their real emotions. They cannot comprehend other people and their own emotions.

- Emotional Outburst

People with low emotional quotient have a problem with controlling their emotions. They often get emotional outbursts that lack control.

- They Have a Problem in Maintaining Friendships

They have a problem with keeping friends because they always portray a picture of being abrasive. Friendships require compassion and sharing of emotions, which is a problem for people with low cmpathic quotient.

Finding the Right Level of Empathy

If our test above showed that you have low levels of empathy, you should not despair; there is still hope. You are lucky because empathy is a muscle and not inherited. Let us find out different ways you can boost your empathy level.

- Find situations that require empathy and take advantage to show empathy.

- There are many opportunities to show your empathic side; never ignore any one of them, but it is important to be in control of your own emotions first.

- Train yourself to have good listening skills. When you are listening to a person, focus all your attention on what they are saying and validate their feelings. Do not make judgmental comments but instead make comments like, "It must be painful. You are a strong person indeed".

- Train yourself to be an observer and do not involve yourself in any situation emotionally and psychologically.

- When encountered with a difficult situation, direct all your focus on the problem but never on the consequent emotions from the problem.

- When you find yourself in a situation where you need to listen to other people's problems, you should acknowledge their feelings and at the same time, guard yours to remain with you only. If the situation makes you feel guilty, control that feeling, especially if the problem was not as a result of your actions or words.

- Train yourself to apologize only when you have wronged the other party and not because you are feeling remorseful for their problems.

- Give genuine reactions. Your reactions must be a replica of your facial expressions.

- Challenge yourself. Indulge in challenging activities that push your limits. You can learn a new language or learn to play a musical instrument. By doing the above things, they humble you, and as a result, you increase your empathy level.

- Travel- Travel to a new place, meet new people, and learn about their culture. It gives you the ability to start appreciating others.

- Feedback- There is no better way to learn than hearing from a second unbiased source. Ask your family and friends on your interaction skills and check with them once in a while to see if you are improving.

- Fit yourself in other people's shoes. Talk to other people about their life challenges and troubles and at the same time, ask how they felt after sharing with you.

Chapter 6. Healing Through Establishing a Hygienic Routine

Empathic people sense and obtain other people's liveliness, which might be quite challenging. The senses of an empath might be enhanced, and the observation of life might be irresistible. A stroll into the park or hanging out with acquaintances might be strenuous. Generally, a range of aspects, comprising the surroundings and group you meet, influences the physical and psychological wellbeing. This assumption is not correct for everybody; however, it is an exceptional one for people with empathy and the over-sensitive ones.

When you are a compassionate person, you are attached to the hurting of other individuals, trying to hang on it as your own. Keep in mind that there is a lot someone might do to assist other individuals. Empathic people might attempt to assist and direct people as they can, however at the end the individual feeling the pain should be ready to assist him or herself for true healing to happen. Frequently, the caring character blind empaths, consequently people do not desire or are not ready to be assisted since they are happy in the protection of their depression.

There are several steps that empathic people can put into practice to enable them to start the journey of healing.

Disconnection

Detaching from close individuals is tough for empathic people; however, it is the best technique to begin the healing procedure. Move away from people who are closely associated with you for a short period.

Accept

Similarly, to handling tricky situations in life, it is vital that you acknowledge that you are an empathic person. Do not assume the power of acceptance as it is one of the key steps of making progress in troubling situations. There is nothing bad about being an empathic person; the fact is that you are exceptional. People with Empathy are remarkable; however, they have a tendency of thinking that there is something regarding them. People in the world have to take good care of empaths, not empaths taking of other them.

Hold on It

After an empath has accepted that they are empathic, they should make it an ingredient of who they are. Hold on your life and accept who you are. Satisfaction in your compassion is the only means to move from reacting like a casualty of it.

Deliberate

Nobody can highlight enough the significance of contemplation. There are several meditation methods accessible to learn and understand; however, you have to discover what suits you. For instance, white sound or a particular sort of music is the best meditation technique for some people. On the other hand, other people require silence as a means of meditation. It is good to understand what works well for your mind.

Adore It

Accommodating your empathic state and holding on it are vital; however, you have to adore it. You are exceptional because communities in your life are lucky to have you in the society. Being a person with empathy is a part of what forms you.

Create limitations

As an empath seeking to heal, it is significant to create limitations. Let persons in your life live on the other part of that contour, and when they go over it that makes easier for an empath to move them far. One of the toughest sections for people with empathy is booting individuals out of their activities and crossing limitations is an excellent reason.

Hygiene Rituals

Spend time alone on a daily basis

As an empath seeking to heal, you should have your time separately each day; however, if it is not possible to be alone regularly, create your time occasionally. When you can spend time unaccompanied without several communications with other individuals and no exterior interruption, you shall have more energy. In addition, being alone implies that not even being in a similar physical state with other individuals. Spending time alone is significant to an empath as it allows them to recharge their energy. Inform your relatives and acquaintances that spending some time alone is something you require. Assist them to recognize how significant this is for you. When you start spending time alone, you shall see the dissimilarity.

Take a salt and scrubs

It is not an undisclosed that salt attracts unhelpful energy, and from different practices, it helps. Several people prefer using sea and Epsom salt in their bathwater, pooled with indispensable oil of preference. In addition, people do it when they sense they require cleansing. On the other hand, people apply salt cleanse in the bathe to clean residue energy they sense on their bodies. You can make these for yourself, mixing marine salt with emerald or coconut oil. What an empath adore, combine it collectively, and include necessary oils of your preference. You shall feel the distinction. People who live closer to safe oceans can take time to swim because oceans are an ideal source of marine salt.

Refining clean up

Occasionally, water is a fantastic decontaminant. Subsequently, people prefer using it to clear their energy whilst cleaning their bodies. Empaths imagine water rinsing away the energy obtained from other people and the energy they no longer desire to keep. Empaths might also picture a color of their choice while trying to release unwanted energy. Several people prefer visualizing blue or white; however, finding something that works for you is vital during the healing process.

Spend time in the natural world

When you may, relax a tree, contemplate in the recreational area or stroll to rejuvenate. Trees have gorgeous energy that might assist you feel healthier and recharging is pure in a natural setting. Several people established that farming assists as well because you acquire the energy from the ground. Therefore, you are refining and getting fresh energy spontaneously.

Protecting

Empaths should never depart their homes without their energetic guard on. Particularly, if they use municipal means of transport or arrange to intermingle with other group people.

Marking

When applying smudging, empaths might embrace sage or exasperate sticks of preference. Several people use Nag, as they adore the smell and how it usually gives them confidence. If empaths feel, they have obtained a lot of unhelpful energy they require smudging themselves entirely. Occasionally, empaths should do it instinctively as they cannot be erroneous. On the other hand, empathic people should do vertical or spherical actions and function through their chairs.

Sweep

Picture you had a few dust on your top and you wish to sweep it down. This is precisely a similar action. Empathic people should get rid of unconstructive energy. You may feel remains on your arms after getting rid of negative energy, therefore, make sure to clean hands with freezing water after the sweeping procedure.

Visualize

Comparable to the hallucination in the bathing room, sit in contemplation and envisage golden colorless brightness coming from the peak of your skull and cleaning away anything that is trapped on you, transferring it down on the ground. The visualization procedure shall also assist with preparation, which is recommended to assist you feel reasonable.

Avoid the phone and internet

Switch off your telephone and avoid the internet frequently. An empath should read a book or settle down. Occasionally, getting a lot of notices and news from your phone or laptop might be strenuous. The best step is turning off your laptop and switching your phone off and witness your energy increase.

Breathing tasks

Several yoga practices and breathing techniques do wonders to empaths seeking to heal. When removing negative energy from their body, empathic people should use energizing breathing tasks. The breathing practices should be performed in a secure place with the eyes blocked and in small periods, as they are influential. Yoga and breathing practices clear empaths energy and rejuvenate them instantaneously. This practice is realistic and simple to perform anytime you require feeling good.

Daily Routines for Healing an Empath
Morning habit

An empath might get up nourishing his or her uncertainties, doubts, and distress, or he or she might wake up encouraging your happiness and tapping into uncontaminated, constructive energy.

If you are a person with empathy, make a functioning morning schedule. As part of a functioning morning routine, empaths should try offering themselves Reiki and meditation. Putting the above practices into a daily schedule boosts one's body with constructive energy and helps me feel balanced, grounded and in harmony. Generally, it makes the attitude for the entire day and makes an empath less responsive and premeditated. Subsequently, an empath must note a purpose for the day and inscribe it down in their periodical. On the other hand, there should be days when empaths insert extra activities to their morning schedule; however, the Reiki and contemplation are invariable. Generally, the first thing an individual does after waking up is vital, because it influences the outcome of the activities they undertake during the day. If you are an empath seeking to heal and you presently do not have a morning schedule, begin on a small note since little is better than doing nothing. Therapists meet several empaths who have no clue that there is a reference for their hypersensitivity. Empaths understand that they are destined to assist other people and do not know why they are exhausted each time and experience no happiness.

Midday schedule

When you desire to survive as an empowered person of empathy, you should offer yourself authorization to pause, reorganize, and rearrange at midday. Rearranging at dusk is not adequate for an empath seeking to heal. The amounts of energy people obtain from other people amass in their body. Fabricating a midday schedule plays a vital role in ensuring that the acquired energy is released from the body. Irrespective of the duration of refreshment, ensure that at least you go out to get some fresh air. You can take a swift stroll around the building. The air outside the building defuses the unconstructive energy you soak up from other people.

Evening schedule

Late afternoon is when a person desires to spend time contemplating the day's activities and planning for the day ahead. At this point, people have a tendency of awakening their powerhouse that comprises sensitivity, imagination, and instinct. Think of activities you like doing in your free time. Some people find pleasures in drawing while others in singing. If you love drawing, draw some of your favorite images in sand, in books, or on timber. Draw every evening and you shall notice some tremendous changes in your life.

Bedtime habits

Going to bed psychologically stimulated may lead to nervousness. The unease may make you to have sleepless nights. Before retiring to bed, you wish to remove the unnecessary energy that pulls you behind, so your energy is sparkling and your pulsation is excellent. Below are a number of thoughts for a bedtime schedule. People, who find writing enjoyable, make a periodical and release your feelings out on the manuscript. Take some minutes, around ten to twenty, working on yoga and Reiki to let go of the pressure from the mind and body. Use cold water to clean your face, rub the face, your arms, apply the whole body with a moisturizer, and comb your hair gently. Pay attention to calm, shooting songs, and say an appreciation. Say a short prayer to God because it is a spiritual way of staying positive.

Keep in mind that both the hygiene and routine rituals come after ensuring that you have mastered the tricks you require in order to make yourself emotionally safe irrespective of the circumstances. In addition, you might not have the freedom to be capable of totally removing or separating yourself from the stressful actions. However, this is a good technique of making the chance to disconnect from a collection of nervousness and anguish. The technique also plays a vital role in making understandable limits about what you might do and manage against what you cannot handle. At this minute, you may choose if you may concentrate on a dispute or call your close friends. However, putting into practice several routines is significant in ensuring that an empath successfully heals from a stressful life and start living a healthy and more enjoyable one.

Chapter 7. Distinction Between Negative And Positive Empathy

The Empath Personality

Being an empath is a beautiful gift. You are wise and caring, insightful and perceptive. You take care of those you love and have a deep consideration and respect for all life on earth.

It is important when looking into how you can live your best life and thrive psychologically and spiritually that you first have a sound innerstanding of what it truly means to be an empath. There are different levels to being an empath as we will explore in the next section, however, for now, let's break down the empath personality so you can innerstand it holistically.

All of the following are aspects to the empath personality however in varying degrees. For example, there may be elements you strongly resonate with and others which you only see a small part of yourself embodying. This knowledge is not taught in school, nor is it widely accepted, and many unique abilities that accompany being spiritually aware and connected and existing in a higher frequency or vibrational state of being are intuitively felt and innerstood. Your empath nature connects instinctively to something beyond the everyday 'I' and often separation based reality which many people still reside in. Looking at the varying aspects to being an empath, therefore, can be a healing journey in itself.

It is OK if you only resonate with a few. Not all empaths display all of these qualities or characteristics. As you read the different aspects of the empath personality, spark your awareness back to memories or a memory where you may have been displaying some of these abilities without being conscious of what was occurring at the time. With each, there is a description of what it means, followed by how you may have been subconsciously or unconsciously displaying and embodying it.

The Artist, Creative, and Visionary

You are an artist. Due to your ability to connect to something above and beyond you through your deep and rich emotional wisdom and intuitive sight, you can also tune in to universal archetypes, ideas, concepts, and often ingenious images and thoughts in a unique way. This makes you a natural artist, creative, and visionary. Whether you choose to express yourself through song, dance, art, painting, drawing, poetry, writing, photography, film making, or directing, you can achieve great things. The visionary aspect to your nature can, literally, connect on an unseen level to some concept or archetype beyond the physical realm, and further bring it forth into the physical. Alanis Morissette is one of the most well-known empaths and even if you have not yet heard of her, her music inspires many people around the world.

Practical Implications of being the Artist, Creative and Visionary: If you embody the artist, creative, or visionary you may have found yourself as a child daydreaming and letting your mind wander to unseen worlds and ideas. Your imagination was rich and you may have been bored in social or overly externally stimulating situations. You also may have naturally had a strong inner knowing that you could come up with better or ingenious ideas and solutions to ones being presented in school, or by your teachers and peers. Your abstract and creative ways of thinking may not have been appreciated or understood by others.

The Musician, Performer, and Storyteller

Like the artist, creative and visionary, you are a musician, performer, and storyteller. Even if you don't ground this into a career or profession, you still have strong elements of being a performer. Many people naturally assume that to be an empath means to be an introvert yet they are not synergistic. Many empathic people are introverted as there are some strong intrinsic links and associations, however many empaths are also highly extroverted. This is because of your ability to connect and because of your love of connection. Once you find yourself, become centered and begin to live in an empathic and harmonious flow, you will find that using your gifts and personality strengths through poetry, performing, storyteller or by connecting others through musical expression comes naturally to you.

Practical Implications of being the Musician, the Performer, and the Storyteller: You found yourself naturally being able to play music, pick up a drum beat or understand aspects relating to advanced storytelling or performance without being taught. You had an ability to connect to others on a deep level, without teaching, and could easily and almost effortlessly pick up and adopt many roles. You may have related to characters in plays, performers, or musicians in a deeper way unexplained by your mind, and experienced certain music as a transcendental and 'other-worldly' experience.

The Dreamer, Seer, and Psychic

One thing that is not often taught in schools nor accepted mainstream is the fact that you, dear empath, are an extremely gifted person. You are a dreamer - you love to explore your dreams and merge with other worlds. Yet your abilities to merge with the subconscious also lies beyond this. Many empaths have a seer-like quality to them because, as stated, you can connect to some archetype or invisible symbol or idea which transcends the three-dimensional reality.

In addition to actually dreaming and enjoying the world of dreams you also may have the ability to astral travel, astral projection, or lucid dream at will. These are three things which come naturally to many empaths and when you are young you may not be able to explain them. We all have an astral body, an energetic layer of ourselves which extends beyond the physical. This astral layer of existence is responsible for all links and connections to psychic, intuitive, spiritual, and archetypal phenomena. It is also where you can connect to dream worlds and your subconscious during sleep or in that period between waking life and sleep when you are in between the worlds.

Astral travel is the ability to explore some other dimension, dream scenario or world, or altered state of consciousness at will, completely connected to your conscious mind. Astral projection is similar however instead of physically leaving your body and exploring, such as in dreams, you stay connected to your physical being and vibrate at a different frequency. Your mind is allowed to 'project' to some spiritual or multidimensional reality, usually to retrieve insight, wisdom, universal symbols and ideas, or some teachings and lessons being shown by your higher self, otherwise known as the higher mind (we will explore lucid dreaming later in this book).

Practical Implications of being the Dreamer, Seer, and the Psychic: You often had dreams you couldn't explain yet knew were sending you a message or direct insight in some way. You knew this even before reading and learning about what was occurring. If you embody these empath aspects you also have a deep inner feeling regarding people and places. You would 'just know' if somewhere didn't feel right or a person didn't have good energy. You also would know which way to go and which route was the best when on an adventure, exploration, or nature walk. Your dreams may have been vivid and you may even have found yourself become bolted out of or into your body from sleep.

The Healer, Counselor, and Therapist

Because of your unique gifts to connect to others on a deep level, you are a natural healer, counselor, and therapist. Many empaths actually go onto becoming healers, and therapists as these paths and professions are strongly associated with your true nature. As a healer, counselor, or therapist you possess vast levels of compassion, kindness and a genuine desire to help and be of service. You have a wise and empathic nature and are very patient, and with incredible listening skills. People feel comforted, safe, and protected around you, and you tend to live and resonate in your heart chakra. Your heart chakra is known as the central chakra, the energy vortex which links lower self and higher self (we will look at the chakra system in detail later). It is the seat of compassion, kindness, empathy, and a connection to others and the natural world, and having a strong heart chakra enables you to thrive in any healing or counseling profession. You also may be a healer or counselor to your friends and family.

Practical Implications of being the Healer, the Counselor, and the Therapist: You had a unique way of connecting to others on a deep level and may have found strangers coming up to you to talk when in your late teens to early 20s. People had an unexplainable pull to you and knew they could open up to you. You may have had a natural connection with animals and nature and felt most content and at peace in their presence like you weren't being judged and could be yourself. You also may have been intrinsically drawn to quantum physics, eastern mythology or Buddhism books and had strong inner recognition of the significance of holistic health and alternative medicine.

The Carer, Social or Support Worker, and Companion

Connected to being a natural healer, counselor, and therapist is your inner tendencies to taking on a caring and supporting role. Many of the caregivers, social and support workers, and companions you see today are either empaths or have strong empathic tendencies. Unlike other characters and personality types, such as narcissists or energy vampires who thrive from taking from others, you thrive from giving and taking on a supportive and caring role. This is essential because of your ability and need for connection. As an empath, you are deeply connected to your environments, surroundings, and other people (and animals), and anything which threatens your connection can lead to pain, struggle, and inner turmoil. As we explore later, this is why it is essential to protect yourself and develop healthy boundaries, and why channeling and expressing these qualities of yours can lead to you living your best and most happy and harmonious life.

Practical Implications of being the Carer, the Social or Support Worker, and Companion: Growing up you may have been particularly shy and introspective and perhaps told you were too sensitive more often than not. This is because you are extremely compassionate and naturally destined to help others in some way, and take on a caring and supporting role. As a child and teenager, you may not have understood this and therefore became shy and quiet as a result. You also may have had strong feelings of wanting to be a vet or the like when asked what you want to be when you are older. Finally, you may have had a strong aversion to violence and became increasingly disturbed when seeing violent or 'hateful' acts and scenes on television or in movies, or when witnessing the suffering of others.

The Animal Whisperer, Charity Worker, and Volunteer

The empath personality is defined by connection, understanding (or now you are aware, innerstanding), and being able to feel what it is like to be another. Many empaths take this ability further and can actually read minds, or at least merge with another on such a level that they know what they are thinking or feeling. This gift can be used in animal whispering. You are a sensitive soul with a big heart, therefore choosing a path or career aligned to helping animals and being a guide or channel for them is a route many empaths choose to take. You tend to feel more comfortable around animals or in nature where you can just be yourself. This is where you along with many empaths not only survive but thrive. Simultaneously many empaths choose to become involved in charity or animal welfare work so this is another direction which you may share a resonance. Essentially any hobby, career, path or direction allowing you to make use of your sensitive, caring, empathic and intuitive gifts will allow you to shine.

Practical Implications of being the Animal Whisperer, Charity Worker, and Volunteer: You may have developed a deep and personal relationship to animals which no one knew about. When visiting zoos, sanctuaries, wildlife areas or parks you could speak to animals on an inner level and felt an emotional and telepathic connection. When coming across a homeless person in the street you have had real and sincere compassion for them, which sometimes translated into pain. You may have also felt different from your family in some unexplainable way.

The Tarot Reader, Spiritual Healer, and Energy Worker

This brings us on to the spiritual stuff. You are deeply spiritual and intuitive, even if you are not yet conscious of it. This can manifest in many 'magical' ways such as knowing what someone is about to say before they say it, sensing an event about to occur, or being able to pull something out of someone hidden deep within. You may be psychic, have precognitive dreams or even visions and may live in an alternate reality together. Many empaths exist in multiple dimensions with one foot in this world and the other in another. This allows you to connect with a higher source or power. Whether you call this god, the goddess, spirit, or the universe, it is very real to you, and when tuning in to connect to these realms you can be a powerful and unique asset in someone's life. You may use your spiritual gifts and awareness to write books, heal others, teach in some way or take on a leadership role. Mother Teresa is a prime example of a spiritual empath who used her gifts in service to others.

Practical Implications of being the Tarot Reader, Spiritual Healer, and Energy Worker: You were deeply drawn to all thing mystical, spiritual and metaphysical from your mid to late teens. You may have been interested in quantum physics, crystals, astrology, supernatural abilities, and ancient wisdom. You possessed a deep knowing of all things and could see beyond people's hidden motives, feelings, and intentions. You may have begun meditating at a young age, and reading spiritual literature or wisdom infused books on the occult, spiritual or metaphysical topics. Your dreams may have been vast and profound and you may have naturally begun to astral project or lucid dream. All of your senses become heightened and your love for animals and mother earth increased with the more knowledge you acquired.

The Independent Worker and 'Self-Employed One'
Because of your inherent dislike of certain characters, roles, interactions, and energies you are most suited to self-employment or highly independent roles. This can manifest in a number of ways such as through being a self- employed plumber, electrician, handywoman or man or owning your own small business. The main point with this is that you have an aversion and furthermore extreme sensitivity to certain noises

which come with 'normal' jobs. Working in an office, for example, can be extremely stressful and even harmful to your empathic nature, as can working in sales or any job where you have to interact with a large number of people on a daily basis.

Practical Implications of being the Independent Worker and Self- Employed One: You had a particular aversion in school to certain topics and perspectives taught as truth. You were not necessarily an outward rebel but you were an inward one, and frequently went against the norm. Structure and oppressive ways made you feel limited and you preferred to come up with your own creative solutions and ways of thinking than following set orders. Rules and regulations may have seemed oppressive to you and your political views may have been strongly steered towards liberalism.

Although these are not the different types of empath becoming aware of the varying aspects to the empath personality and your nature can really aid in your journey of discovery and self-development. Empathy is an encompassing gift and its applications are vast. Inner and understanding yourself may just be the key to your own personal puzzle!

Chapter 8. Empaths and Work

As an empath, you will face particular challenges in the workplace. Everyone deserves a job that fits their abilities and personality, but you need to take extra care before accepting a position because a toxic work environment can make you emotionally, spiritually, and physically sick – fast. So, as an empath, how can you pick the right kind of job and thrive at work?

Always Ask For A Workplace Tour Before Accepting A Role

When you go for an interview, ask whether you can take a tour if someone hasn't already offered to show you around. Pay attention to the employees' facial expressions, their body language, and the way they talk to one another. You'll quickly surmise whether the organization is toxic. Unless you are in desperate need of money, follow your gut instinct and avoid workplaces that contain a significant amount of negative energy.

Pay close attention to the lighting, the noise levels, the amount of clutter, and the layout of the desks. Ask yourself whether you could be comfortable working in such an environment, from both a physical and emotional perspective. A high salary might be enticing, but your health and sanity must come first. Even if other people tell you that a job is too good an opportunity to pass up, trust your intuition.

You have the power to make a positive difference in the workplace, but you are under no obligation to sacrifice your mental and physical health if doing so is beyond your comfort zone. Never feel bad about choosing the right job for you.

Use Your Gift As A Selling Point

Empaths are not show-offs by nature, and the prospect of selling yourself in a job interview might be enough to make you feel queasy. But think of it this way – your empathic qualities are actually an increasingly valuable commodity in the workplace. We tend to associate the business world, and even the public sector, with a kind of cut-throat mentality where everyone is trying to outdo one another and compete for the best positions and the most money.

However, our society is increasingly aware that taking care of one another and our planet is the only way forward. We still have a long way to go in creating a more caring world but, in general, we are starting to understand the benefit of a healthy work-life balance and the merit of cooperative working practices rather than a dog-eat-dog mentality. If you feel up to the challenge, you can use your gift to help drive this change!

You know that there is far more to life – and work – than status or salary. Your gift makes you perfectly suited to roles that require listening, conflict resolution, and mentoring skills.

Psychiatrist, author, and empath Dr. Judith Orloff maintains that empaths bring passion, excellent communication skills, and leadership ability to their professional roles. When an interviewer asks what you can bring to a job, don't hesitate to give examples of times you have demonstrated these gifts.

Working Alone Versus Working With Others

Although you have strong leadership potential, a role involving extensive contact with colleagues and customers on a day-to-day basis may prove too draining, especially if you are not yet confident in your ability to handle negative energy and toxic individuals. Be honest with yourself when applying for a position. If it entails working as part of a busy team with few opportunities to recharge during the day, think carefully before making an application.

Most empaths are well suited to working for themselves or taking on jobs within small organizations. Working in a large office or noisy environment may be too stimulating – and that's fine! We all have different needs and talents, so do not allow anyone to make you feel inferior for not being able to handle a "normal" workplace. As an empath, you may quickly become overwhelmed by the prospect of having to interact with coworkers, members of the management team, and customers.

On the other hand, working alone can result in social isolation if you take it to extremes. If you decide to run a small business from home, for example, be sure to schedule some time with family and friends at least a couple of times per week.

Not only do you need to nurture your relationships, but it is also helpful to gain an outsider's perspective on your work from time to time. Sometimes, you may get so caught up in a project that relatively minor problems seem to take on a life of their own. Talking to other people allows you to take a more realistic view and help you come up with new solutions.

If Your Environment Drains Your Energy, Ask For Reasonable Adjustments

You can't expect your boss to redecorate the office just to suit your preferences or to fire an energy vampire, but you can ask them politely whether they would mind making a few small adjustments. For example, if there is a harsh strip light directly over your desk, you could ask whether it would be possible to turn off the light and use softer, gentler lamps instead.

If you work in an environment in which people talk loudly, experiment with white noise or other sound recordings designed to trigger feelings of calm and emotional stability. Try sounds recorded in nature, as these are often soothing for empaths. You can find lots of free resources on YouTube or specialized noise-generating sites such as mynoise.net. If possible, listen to natural or white noise via noise-cancellation headphones for at least a portion of your workday.

There are also additions and adjustments you can make that do not require permission from your boss. For instance, you can place crystals on your desk as a means of countering negative energy and set aside a few minutes each day – even if you are incredibly busy – to ensure your desk is clear of unnecessary clutter. If you work with a computer, pick a calming scene or color as your desktop wallpaper. Frame a photo or uplifting picture and keep it on your desk. Look at it for a few seconds when you need a dose of positive energy.

If you enjoy your job but would prefer to spend less time around other people, consider asking your manager whether you can work from home a couple of days each week. This can give you some respite from other peoples' energy and enables you to take a break at any time. Working from home comes with the privilege of setting up an environment that suits you perfectly. For example, you could install a water feature on your desk or play natural background noise throughout the day without fear of eliciting annoying questions from your coworkers.

Watch Out For Energy Vampires

If you come across an energy vampire in your personal life, you usually have the option of cutting contact with them, or at least limiting how much time the two of you spend hanging out. Unfortunately, this isn't the case when you are forced to work alongside them.

This is where boundaries come into play. You need to politely but firmly assert yourself from the outset of your professional relationship. Don't be drawn into petty workplace gossip, and don't accept any invitations from toxic people to socialize outside of work. Draw on your best energy self-defense skills, and always put your wellbeing before professional obligations.

Empaths who choose to work in the helping professions, whether with other people or animals, need to remain aware of the effect of their work on their energy levels. For example, if you work as a psychologist or therapist, speaking to a client who is going through an especially sad or difficult time in their life can leave you exhausted, depleted, and even depressed. Be sure to allow a few minutes between clients or appointments in which to ground yourself, and schedule plenty of time to relax and nurture yourself outside of work.

Draw A Line Between Your Workplace and Home

If you work outside the home, it's a good idea to devise a routine that creates a clear dividing line between your professional and personal life. As an empath, you are susceptible to carrying the negative energy of others with you. You may catch yourself worrying not only about the problems you are facing at work, but also those of your colleagues, bosses, and customers. Unless you learn how to "switch off," you will soon become overwhelmed, anxious, and depressed.

When it's time to wrap up your work for the day, stay mindful of the transition between work and home. Create a ritual that automatically encourages you to switch your focus to personal interests and feelings rather than those of colleagues and clients. For example, you may wish to spend the final five minutes of your workday in meditation or tidying your desk whilst listening to a particular soundtrack or piece of music. If you have a friend or relative who always raises your energy levels, you could get into the habit of texting them just before leaving work or on the way home.

Focus On How Your Work Helps Others

It isn't always possible to change your job or work in the field of your choosing. If you are stuck in a job that isn't right for you and are in no position to make a change any time soon, try approaching your work with a new mindset.

As an empath, you have a talent for helping others. Not only do they benefit from your support, but you also get to soak up their positive energy too. It's truly a win-win situation! Try to find opportunities to lend a hand to someone else, and offer emotional support as long as it doesn't leave you feeling too drained.

For example, if one of your colleagues seems especially stressed, take the initiative and ask them if they'd like to talk to you for five minutes about anything that's bothering them. Sometimes, just offering a listening ear can turn someone's day around! Or perhaps you could offer a more practical form of help. For instance, you could offer to take everyone's mail to the mailroom on your coffee break. Acts of service and kindness allow you to find a sense of meaning in your work, even if you are hoping to change careers in the near future.

Chapter 9. How to Lead a Normal Life as an Empath

Many people with empathic personality experience significant difficulties in trying to lead a normal life. This is because; such people are usually consumed by the issues affecting other people in society and within their immediate family settings. As an empath, you might find yourself spending too much time thinking about an unfortunate event that someone you know has experienced or even an event that has taken place some place far away. Furthermore, you will constantly feel like you have to take action in order to assist an individual around you or contribute towards a greater course. Your predisposition to help and care for other people might undermine your capacity to lead a normal life. Be that as it may, they are things that you can do in order to enable you to lead a normal life despite your empathic nature.

Know that there is nothing wrong with you

The fact that you are more concerned about things a little bit more than the average person does not mean that there is something wrong with you. It is important to note that no two people are the same and that you are a unique entity just like everyone else.

In order to ensure that you lead a normal life as a person with an empathic nature, you should not try to hide your true self. Do not try to fit into what you think is your definition of a normal person because, in the real sense, normal is something that is extremely relative. You might consider your personality to be different based on what one person has said to you but you end meeting another person who considers you to be normal. Leading an ordinary life will call for an unconditional acceptance of who you are and constantly reminding yourself that there is nothing wrong with you. If you are able to do so, then you will be at ease with yourself and this will make other people to be at ease with you. Other people will, for instance, find it much easier to interact with you which a very big part of a life that is considered normal. Furthermore, you will not end up feeling as if you are superior to other people because they do not seem to see what you see. You will instead, treat others as normal but slightly different in terms of their personality. This will, in turn, make others accept you for who you are making it easier for you to lead a normal life.

Stay off the News

First and foremost, in order to lead a normal life as an empath, you should try and stay off the conventional news outlets. The media is awash with news networks that are meant to inform and educate the general public. However, a significant amount of news out there usually relates to tragic events such as road accidents, natural calamities such as earthquakes and tsunamis, terrorist attacks and other such events. Continues bombardment by such news can have very detrimental effects on a person with empathic nature. This is because; your natural inclination to care and assist other people will make you feel like you have to do something. The truth of the matter is you cannot help everyone. In fact, some of these events might be taking place in places that are very far away from you. You will, therefore, end up feeling helpless and hopeless which might eventually lead to depression.

In order to lead a normal life as empathy, you should try and control what you see in mainstream news and media outlets. It might not be possible to completely stay off the news especially in this era of new media and social media platforms, but you can certainly control the same. For instance, you can choose to mainly select entertainment channels on your TV instead of spending too much time on news channels such as CNN or Aljazeera. Similarly, you can unsubscribe from new media channels and social media platforms that keep bombarding you with sad news. By doing so, you will not be exposed to a lot of unfortunate events affecting other people thus reducing the amount of time you will have to spend thinking about others and what you can do in order to save them. Furthermore, you will have more time to concentrate on your immediate family members and this will make it much easier for you to lead a normal life.

Put Yourself First

One way of ensuring that you are able to lead a normal life as an empath is constantly remembering to put yourself first. Your empathic nature implies that you will most often than not be tempted to put the needs and aspirations of other people before your own. In fact, some people may recognize this behavior and try to deliberately take advantage of you. These people are referred to as emotional vampires and they can undermine your potential to be successful in life.

Within the modern-day world, it is not sustainable to put the needs of other people before your own. Your empathic nature is a girt that ought to be utilized. However, you can only help other people if you are stable, both financially and emotionally. Putting yourself first is the most effective way of attaining success in your life. Once have become successful, then it will be much easier for you to take care and assist other people in whatever way they need you. For instance, you might be having a sick relative but spending too much time thinking about their situation will not help. The only way that can help is by availing the money that they will require for medical care. You will only have such funds if you are financially stable as a result of prioritizing your own needs before the needs of other people.

Appreciate Your Limitations

It is important to appreciate the fact that no single human being can save the world. Put in plain terms, you cannot be the solution to everything that affects the people around you. There will always be those situations where you can comfortably assist and those where you simply cannot do anything. For this reason, it is important to establish personal boundaries so as to lead a normal life as a person with empathic nature. Limitations in this context relates to having an understanding regarding those situations where you can be of help to someone else. For instance, depending on your financial situation, you can have an idea with respect to the maximum amount of money you can spend in order to assist other people in need. Similarly, your boundaries can also relate to the maximum duration of time you can set aside outside your normal schedule in order to assist another person.

Setting boundaries and abiding by them will ensure that you always have something for yourself. For instance, boundaries regarding the maximum amount of money you can use to help others will ensure that you have the much-needed monetary resources for your own needs and the needs of your dependents. This will enable you and your dependents to lead normal lives notwithstanding your empathic nature.

Limit Your Level of Responsibility

As an empath, it is important to accept the fact that you cannot be responsible for each and every person in your life. This implies that you should not spend too much time worrying about other people since, at the end of the day, they will always be someone in need. In order to lead a normal life, you should pay more attention instead to the people who you are directly responsible for such immediate family, close friends and a few extended family members. When you to this, you will always set aside time and money to attend to the needs of the people who really matter and care about you. It is rather pointless to spend too much time worrying about hunger and disease problems affecting a third world nation when your child does not have enough to eat.

At of the day, you have to know that one way you can contribute towards solving the problems affecting other people is by first and foremost addressing the problems that you face. It is the collective responsibility of all human beings to make the world a better place. Such a huge responsibility can never be left to one person or a few individuals whether they are empaths or not. Making the world a better place might seem an ambiguous expression or a grand task however, it can be a very simple thing to do if you know what it entails. On an individual level, making the world a better place should simply entail caring for the people and the environment around you. For instance, you should ensure that your family is well catered for in terms of their daily needs, healthcare requirements and even life improvement opportunities. Similarly, you should ensure that you take measures to enhance your immediate physical environment such as participating in communal tree planting exercises, exercising proper waste disposal, recycling and such activities. If each and every person is able to do those simple things, then the world will indeed be a better place. There would fewer people dying of hunger and various diseases, there would fewer natural calamities such as extreme heat waves and tsunamis and other such things that typically preoccupy the mind of an empathic individual.

Share your concerns with others

Your empathic nature implies that you will from time to time worry about things that might not necessarily give other people sleepless nights. This can be a lonely experience when you find that you are the only person concerned about the increasing levels of greenhouse being emitted by various industries or other such issues that seemingly do not worry about the people around you. In such a scenario, you might be tempted to keep your worries and concerns to yourself in order to maintain a seemingly normal outlook. But this is not advisable since such concerns, worries and disappointments might see you implode with negative pent up energy.

As a person with an empath personality, it is advisable to share your concerns with other people, especially whenever you feel strongly about certain things. You might notice that the people around do not seem to care about certain issues but this should not stop you from voicing your concerns. Some people might simply not be well informed about the issue that is troubling you and when you explain to them your concerns, they might appreciate the gravity of the situation. Furthermore, sharing with other people is an outlet avenue that enables you to release that pent-up energy instead of allowing it to pile up and having disastrous consequences at the end.

Appreciate the True Nature of Life

The true nature of life is that in life, there will always be the good, the bad and the ugly. There is nothing that you or anyone else for that matter can do about it. People who have empathic nature will always thrive in the good, but experience difficulties coping with the other two. For instance, you can spend the entire day thinking about why something bad had to happen to someone you know but you may never be able to come up with a definitive answer. The truth is bad things happen to everyone including good people. This is the nature of life and the sooner you accept that, the easier it will be for you to lead your life as an empath.

When you are able to appreciate the true nature of life, you will find it much easier to deal with many of the challenges that you will come across. For instance, you might be better positioned to cope with the fact that one of your loved ones is battling with a terminal illness since you will know that such eventualities are part and [parcel of life. Furthermore, your ability to appreciate the true nature of life will make you much more stable as an empath and you will end up being the rock that other people depend during such difficult times.

Chapter 10. Empath Healing Techniques

Healing Techniques

There are numerous spiritual healing methods that you can use to build up your blessings. Meditation, Reiki, Spiritual Healing gatherings, learning Tarot are only a couple. Discover what is in your general vicinity, join a gathering, read books. On the off chance that you need to build up your blessings, make it your expectation to discover a gathering or instructor in your general vicinity, you'll be flabbergasted how rapidly one will show. Numerous years back, I needed to learn meditation as an approach to build up my spiritual blessings. That very day via the post office, there was a flyer about a course in meditation. Goodness, that was the quickest sign I'd at any point had. It was likewise the course that leads to the improvement of my inborn abilities and blessings, which had recently been covered up.

In case you feel like a fan, you tend to detect and feel the contemplations, emotions and even physical agony of others. Contingent upon the level of your empathic capacities, you may even take on this physical agony without knowing. That is the reason energy mindfulness and establishing are essential components and significant parts of energy clearing.

Energy Clearing Techniques

You can't change the way that you are an empath. This is the means by which you are made at a soul level, and you can't change this spiritual blessing. Some talk of turning on and off being and empathy, it's a little disappointing because it is nonsense to expect that this capacity will be killed on and off. You're aware of what you can do. Being an empath is the kind of person you are, and you are here to figure out how to utilize your empathic blessing as a useful asset for appearance and self-change.

We should plunge into my most helpful spiritual clearing strategies that I use myself as an empath and that I prescribe to my customers:

1. Cutting The Cords

This is a significant assignment that empaths need to turn out to be adept at. Since you are so great at connections and individuals to love you, they likewise remove your energy from you in light of the fact that your energy feels so great, healing, and cherishing. This happens on the grounds that you permitted it without knowing.

At various times associations or etheric lines with relatives, companions, and lovers can, in any case, be available much after the relationship is finished. It's an ideal opportunity to cut the ropes!

To cut lines, essentially think about the individual with which you have had a relationship and envision the string being cut. Promote the person and state the accompanying: "I presently discharge you in love and light."

There are further developed strategies on the most proficient method to cut lines, yet this straightforward technique is as compelling. My assessment is that the more we need to confuse things, the more things get convoluted. It's up to you! My recommendation is to make it straightforward and make it simple. However, do it and do it as often as you feel the need.

For instance, before nodding off every night, ask yourself: "Do I have any connections or lines with anybody that I met today?" Install it and prefer it if you notice it.

Inquire a couple of days after the fact to ensure that the rope has been discharged. You can get professional help if you don't know or think the rope is still there. I frequently find ropes linked to or linked to one of the energy fields.

2. Your psychological body is continually connecting with the psychological assemblage of others, so you get antagonistic contemplations from others.

You additionally make your very own contemplations, and a significant number of them may not be in arrangement with your most elevated great. Know about the accompanying kind of musings:

- Negative

- Redundant

- Repetitive

- Automatic

In the event that you need to find out about your reasoning, examples convey a scratch pad with you and record every one of the contemplations that you have inside a 24 hours time frame. You will be shocked by the fact that it is so difficult to monitor your considerations!

At the point when your musings are sure you adjust to positive vibrations, and you make healing, equalization, and amicability. At the point when they are negative, they make opposition and blockages.

Negative idea structures can be nourished for a considerable length of time, particularly when associated with a horrible encounter.

These negative idea structures are made by negative understanding and desires. The more power you give, the more energy you receive and the more their effect on your equalization condition has been based.

They can be founded on supposition and desires for others. All things considered, they can stall out in your mind and happen again and again undetected, until you start to focus and effectively choose to watch your idea patters.

Contemplations who are made out of dread, melancholy, dread, fault, and outrage they stay appended to your energy field and cause you to vibrate increasingly more in arrangement with these sorts of energies. After some time, they cause you to attract these very encounters throughout your life.

To clear this example, take a gander at your life and check whether you are attracting circumstances you don't care for. In the event that you do, you are some way or another vibrating in arrangement with them without your conscious mindfulness.

Your assignment is to check in with your energy field a few times during the day, in particular, if you feel drained and discouraged, check if you have or have made any negative ideas and consciously let them go.

This is the thing that I typically state:

"I am responsible for my brain, my emotions, and my body."

"I am a processor, amplificator, and transmuter of energy."

"I process my energy to get the hang of, enhancing the positive, and transmuting the negative."

As you state this, imagine a silver-white light purifying your energy field from any trash of thought-frames that are starting to grab hold. This assignment will just take 1 moment to do.

I'm asking you primarily to be calm!

3. Adjusting Your Chakras

Chakra adjusting for empaths is an absolute necessity, and it's an everyday practice. Two times per day, morning, and nights, you have to take a couple of moments to wash down your chakras.

I like to just imagine the accompanying meditation:

Imagine each chakra being purified, re-stimulated, and re-adjusted.

Imagine the whole chakra framework like turning wheels while permitting negative energy out of the body and positive energy inside the body.

With your mind, the eye sees and fell energy streaming and flowing in immaculate equalization and agreement.

4. Make A Sacred Space

This is so significant for everybody, except particularly in the event that you are an empath. A consecrated space can be any area in your home where you can be without anyone else's input and see a spot as completely self-communicated.

This could be your specialty room, your meditation room, or basically your office. This spot must be yours and yours alone. Try not to impart this space to other people (indeed, your children and pets can come in and out!). It doesn't need to be inside; it tends to be outside.

Be imaginative with this, however, locate a unique spot for you to go at any rate once per day. If you are afraid that you can't make a real space, just think of it and go there. What you can do in your brain will astonish you.

A few people end up in the open country, others along the coastline, a desert island, a healing sanctuary; others see themselves on different planets, out in space, or a spaceship made completely of light energy.

5. Smirching Yourself And Your Environment

I love this part, and it is an unquestionable requirement, particularly when you feel down, dismal, or on edge. Smirching your energy field and the earth truly transmutes negative energies from your energy field.

Do this often, particularly the opportunity to feel aligned with your psychological, mental and physical body under the conditions. You are not at all likely. Utilize white sage. Likewise, remember to smirch your home routinely to keep the energy of your living space crisp and clean.

6. Associate With Nature

For anyone who feels overpowered by emotional pressure and mental anguish, nature gives the best type of energy healing accessible. It is my conviction that empaths are here right now to help the vivacious frequencies important to clean the planet.

Most negative musings and negative emotions are conveyed by people. Along these lines, in the event that you are an empath proceed to invest energy in nature alone in any event once per day to energize, you will enable nature to rinse you. Touching a tree can assist you with establishing and wipe out undesirable energies from your body.

Interfacing with animals, blooms, floods of water, and characteristic scenes is the most relieving energy healing treatment you can get.

Sit on the floor against the storeroom of a tree with your back, or walk with your feet exposed to draw positive energy from the earth. This technique is called a set-up or a calming method, which will make you feel fantastic.

7. Utilize Protective Stones

I don't accept that we should be always worried about protection since I accept that we are the main expert in our life. Accepting that we need consistent protection can attract the negative considerations of debilitation, dread, and victimhood.

So as to ensure your energy field, you should know about your energy.

I do accept that empaths need to discover approaches to keep themselves grounded and purified constantly. This is, as I would like to think, the best type of protection.

After the Heart-Wall clearing, it's imperative to put a shield of protection around the hear so as to keep the heart totally protected and ensured structure negative energies and consistently in arrangement with positive energies. When you have cleared your Heart-Wall and put a shield of protection, you should simply enact your shield.

At the point when I work with individuals, I educate just energy procedures that they can use to ensure their auric field, yet I don't advance the requirement for protection as much as the requirement for energy mindfulness.

At the point when we are consciously mindful of our energy, we can't fall casualties of others except if we permit it. Your energies should be continually moving in doing what we are here to do as empaths: process, transmute and intensify the energy. In the event that you are not doing this throughout the day, you will feel stale energy. This is often why you fall back into the negative part of your blessings and feel the need to protect them.

In this way, working with gems and stone encourages you to remain focused and mindful of what's happening in your life. This isn't anything but difficult to do when you are out there, in reality, making your background. In any case, you need not free core interest. Be over your energy!

Obsidian stones are amazing negative energy repellents. You can hold them in or out of your pocket.

Dark Obsidian is valuable in purging your auric field from pessimism. It is utilized to battle off the psychic assault. On the off chance that you do spiritual healing work, this gemstone can assist you with establishing you to the planet Earth.

Scrub your stones as often as possible and program them for healing and protection.

8. Use Journaling, Art, and Drawing

Empaths will, in general, be exceptionally imaginative and love communicating their very own ability when they feel extraordinary. At the point when they don't feel incredible, they will, in general, oppose their masterful capacities since craftsmanship necessitates that they work with their feelings, and this can often cause torment.

I welcome you to think about utilizing craftsmanship as a type of healing and emotional discharge to help you out of parity when you feel stuck.

9. Cry As A Form Of Emotional Release

Empaths have an extremely refined emotional body, and they have to cry when they want to do as such. Crying has such a large number of healing advantages. The vibration of crying fills in the as a purifying instrument for your quality. Kids do this constantly.

Doing Yoga, Tai Chi or different types of energy development can be extremely useful to help discharge pressure, let go of undesirable negative energies, scrub the emanation and realign the body and chakra framework.

Additionally, doing energy work is the ideal approach to keep your atmosphere scrubbed and in concordance with your spirit's way.

10. Ocean Salt Baths

Ocean salt has astounding purifying capacities. Ocean salt coaxes energy out. Having a hot shower containing ocean salt when you feel vigorously overpowered can truly have an enormous effect in the manner you feel. You can utilize standard ocean salt, Himalayan salt, Epsom salt, or other.

A few drops of basic oil can also be included in the water. In the event that you have hypersensitivities, make a point to test them first. Rosemary, citronella and eucalyptus are the best fundamental oils to use for air purification.

What is the best method for energy clearing?

I would urge starting today to receive a portion of these techniques and test with them. Perceive how your body feels. Focus on your emotions and musings. Tune in to your body, what messages is your body sending you? Know about what's going on in your condition.

Notice what individuals state around you and what you state around them and what kind of discussion are you taking part in. Your outside experience is constantly an immediate sign of what's going on in your psyche.

Empathy Knows To Other People's Hearts

Where Has Our Ability to Empathize Gone?

Empathy is simply the capacity to emotionally place into another person's point of view the ability to share and comprehend the feelings, emotions, and viewpoint experienced by someone else, both contrary and constructive. Empathy is the distinguishing proof and relationship that interfaces us as individuals.

We show empathy through proclamations, for example, "I can see you are extremely awkward about this," and "I can comprehend why you would be disturbed." We show empathy through an embrace, a consoling touch, and even through a "high five" when our empathy identifies with somebody's prosperity.

Empathy isn't a similar emotion as compassion. Where empathy enables us to vicariously understanding and relate to other's feelings, compassion is a having of sympathy or distress for the feelings of others. With empathy, we feel with another person, with compassion, we feel for another person.

There are numerous hypotheses concerning the nature versus sustaining part of empathic advancement. Are a few people brought into the world ethically, and a few people brought into the world shrewdness?

Dr Paul Zak has examined the natural premise of good versus detestable conduct over various years and has made an exceptionally intriguing revelation. He found that when individuals feel for others, the pressure triggers the cerebrum to discharge a synthetic called oxytocin. Moreover, an investigation at Berkely inferred that a specific variation of the oxytocin receptor quality is related to the characteristic of human empathy. In the examination, the individuals who had this quality variation were found to have a progressively empathic nature. Dr Zak says this study shows that a handful of people, about 5% of our population, can have a quality variation that makes them less empathic. Finally, some people are not quite sensitive to oxytocin, he said. At the end of the day.

So, there is logical proof that the decency characteristic is encoded in our qualities. In any case, nature isn't the main affecting variable. We might be brought into the world with the ability to have empathy. However, our capacity to apply it, to mind and comprehend, is scholarly conduct.

Social analysts state that empathetic conduct is worked from the protected connection babies create with their folks or essential guardians, and by demonstrating their folks' empathetic conduct towards them and others. Earnest empathetic conduct creates in kids whose guardians continually show, educate, and strengthen it. It is a steady rise that happens with consistency, and minding appeared to them during the developmental long periods of their social and emotional improvement. As a rule, yet not all, grown-ups who need empathy have been casualties of youth manhandle or disregard.

The individuals who have had amazingly excruciating childhoods, ones that have included emotional, sexual, or physical maltreatment, often put some distance between their own feelings while closing themselves off from the torment. Their immature adapting aptitudes leave them burdened with trouble, regardless of whether their own or others and their absence of capacity to encounter their own torment, keeps them from feeling the agony of others. As grown-ups, their intricately assembled protection systems square blame and disgrace while likewise obstructing their conscience. They live through dread, dangers, discipline, and confinement as opposed to empathy and graciousness.

As a rule, the inverse is genuine. The individual over-relates to others' agony, is overpowered by it and turns out to be excessively empathetic to the point that they assimilate the feelings of everybody around them. Their inner torment and enduring are activated when they see others in agony and enduring, thusly become engrossed with every other person's torment and make it their own. I did that for a large portion of my life. Often it was to avoid my own agony; however, amusingly, it made me endure more. I had extremely poor adapting aptitudes, and my boundaries were lopsided if existent by any stretch of the imagination. I likewise displayed the conduct I saw as a youngster.

I do feel that generally speaking, my age, it is more empathetic than age that depends on the relationship with humans, age where families have seen families and friends on the basis of the fact that nothing else has been to do every Sunday.

Truth be told, The University of Michigan's new educational examination annually includes cases that undergraduates who began their school after 2000 had a 40% less empathy compared to undergraduates 30 years earlier. The University of Michigan researchers in the Psychology Society. The most honed drop happened over the most recent nine years. The examination incorporates information from more than 14,000 understudies.

One explanation this is going on is on the grounds that understudies are turning out to be progressively self-arranged as their reality turns out to be progressively increasingly aggressive. Some state that person to person communication is making an increasingly narcissistic age. As indicated by lead analysts, it is more earnestly for the present undergrad to empathize with others on the grounds that such a large amount of their social connections are done through a PC or phone and not through genuine collaboration. With their companions online, they can single out who they will react to and who they will block out. That is more than liable to continue into reality.

This is additionally an age that grew up playing computer games. Quite a bit of their developmental year's advancement has been affected by a contribution from PC created pictures and vicious digital communications. There must be an association. This may mostly clarify the desensitizing of this age.

Another perspective was exhibited by Christopher Lasch, a notable American history specialist, moralist, and social pundit, in a book he distributed in 1979 called, The Culture of Narcissism: American Life during a time of Diminishing Expectations. Lasch joins the predominance of narcissism in our general public to the decrease of the nuclear family, loss of guiding principle, and long haul social breaking down in the twentieth century.

The progressive and idealizing way of life of the 1960s provided a way to look for auto consciousness in the 1970s. He agreed. In all events, people were ineffective in trying to find themselves. A general public that praised self-articulation, trust and self-esteem began to develop. That is fine and dandy, or so it appears, However, more narcissism has been incidentally done because of the middle. Everything has exploded with retrospective hostility, realism, lack of thinking about others, and superficial qualities.

There is surely a considerable lot of us who have not become along these lines reads represent society when all is said in done.

Today we live with steady inward and outside weights of life. Every day our general public faces fear based oppression, wrongdoing, financial emergencies, across the board work weakness, war, political defilement. We see the crumbling of profound quality in any place we look.

What's more, what has befallen our legitimate framework?

The privileges of the culprit have been shown time and time again to take a second room to the privileges of the offenders. In order to control breakers, our laws do almost no. It seems like crooks rule the law, it's telling the truth. If a question of empathy could spike at any moment in a seemingly ordinary human unimaginable wildness, this is an ideal opportunity right now.

Researchers have examined empathy from numerous methodologies and together have discovered both physiological and psychological roots for it. Since people are made out of body, brain, and soul, that bodes well. Numerous things impact our practices.

Simon Baron-Cohen, the 1960's genetic and normal aspects of empathy were investigated by Master in formative psychopathology and chemical imbalances. A New Theory of Cruelty is an explanation of his findings, meetings and discoveries. The aim of the book is to illustrate a way to understand why people do terrible things. In his teaching, he discusses the unpalpable notion of intent and presents an increasingly reasonable hypothesis of compassion and that it occurs in a number of ways.

Aristocrat Cohen says that an individual's degree of empathy originates from an empathy circuit lying profoundly inside the mind. The capacity of this circuit figures out where an individual falls inside the empathy range. He gauges an individual's degree of empathy by degrees, six degrees being an advanced empathy circuit, and zero degrees a low working one.

He orders individuals who have psychopathic and narcissistic character issues, the individuals who come up short on the capacity to feel others' feelings and can't self-control their medications of others, as zero-negative.

The best and most regular way that empathy is evaluated, with empathy characterized as "the responses of one individual to the watched encounters of another," is through a poll called The Interpersonal Reactivity Index. The poll utilizes 5-point scales (A = doesn't portray me well to E = depicts me quite well). This scale is utilized to assess an individual's point of view of himself or herself.

There are four classifications of evaluation. The main classification is Fantasy, as in the announcement, "When I am reading a fascinating story or novel, I envision how I would feel if the occasions in the story were transpiring. The subsequent classification is Perspective-taking, as in the announcement, "Before reprimanding someone, I attempt to envision how I would feel in the event that I was in their place." The third classification is empathetic worry, as in the announcement, "When I see somebody being exploited, I feel sort of defensive towards them." And the fourth class is close to home trouble, as in the announcement, "When I see somebody who seriously needs assistance in a crisis, I turn out badly."

Since empathy starts with the consciousness of someone else's feelings and responsiveness to the unpretentious prompts that others emit, which happen to be capacities that ladies are naturally proficient at, females, for the most part, score higher on these sorts of tests.

The individuals who have encountered the amplest scope of emotions and the individuals who are most in touch with their feelings are likewise progressively ready to empathize with what others feel. These individuals are not commonly a danger to society. Yet, there are likewise individuals who are total without empathy. These are the individuals that are threats to our general public. They are ticking time bombs that may detonate whenever.

Chapter 11. Empath Self-Care Tips at a Glance

Fill your life with good people, good experiences and quality time all to yourself, and practice extreme self-care

Take regular salt baths with essential oils, baking soda, Himalayan salt and/or Epsom salts

Spend a lot of time getting to know any potential partners before becoming physically intimate with them

Spend time pottering, mediating, reading and generally restoring yourself after clearing your energy. Set your expectation to live at a higher level of freedom, peace and joy, rather than simply existing in eternal fight or flight mode, careening from one energy-clearing emergency to the next

Begin to release toxic people from your life or spend as little time with them as possible

Before you go to sleep each night, take an energy inventory and release any stuck energy of anger, fear or sadness you may have picked up from others throughout the day. Try not to carry it with you through the night and into the next day. Release it and start again. Tomorrow is another day!

Never, ever allow yourself to be rushed into a decision of any kind. You are absolutely entitled to say you need more time to think about an offer, and anyone pushing you to make a hasty decision in a very short space of time is a definite red flag

Close your eyes and sense the energy in your home. See if there are any rooms or areas you feel drawn to. If you feel depressed, angry or uncomfortable in your home for no reason, ask your higher self and your energy radar to guide you to the places and spaces that most need clearing

Regularly cleanse the energy in your home using sage to smudge or essential oils in a burner. Play sacred music as you work, and open the windows and doors for a while to allow the fresh, clean air to blow in, washing any lower energies harmlessly away on the cleansing breath of mother nature

Spend three days eating only savoury food, allowing only the occasional green apple for sweetness and see what changes. Retrain yourself to prefer savoury and sour tastes such as green apples and lemon-water.

Squirt lemon juice over everything – lemon juice can help to reduce sugar cravings and who knows, you might learn to love the taste

Find other ways to comfort yourself, and learn to see food as fuel rather than a way to stuff down unpleasant feelings

Strike food off the list of things you use to celebrate or reward yourself.

The only butter in your house should be Shea butter

Before you run to the shops to buy chocolate and sweeties, ask yourself what just happened? Why am I suddenly doing this after weeks of abstinence? Stop, breathe, clear your energy and reach for a green apple. At this point, your body just wants something, anything, to take away the pain and move it out of this horrible toxic state, replacing the stolen energy with some kind of sugar. Train yourself to reach for a green apple when these situations arise. You'll be shocked to see that it can actually work after a while

Do as many things as you can to have fun without food and find fun people to do them with.

Spend more time with people who have a healthier, non-addictive approach to food and nutrition. Watch and learn

Find hobbies you feel passionate about, and which keep you too occupied to think about food

Give yourself plenty of time to get ready for work and cultivate a habit of arriving at appointments early. It's much better to be too early and sit reading calmly while you wait, than to panic and end up taking the underground, getting trapped in a lift with a vampire or generally arriving in a stressed-out panic

Stay away from angry, violent and argumentative people

Join a dance class or take up another hobby that generates happy chemicals in your brain and allows you to shake of negative energy quickly

Switch off the TV and mainstream radio as much as possible and fill your ears with positive, inspirational and education input

As much as possible, weave little time and space treats and structures into your day, and build them into your life

Take naps – guilt free

Remember, there's no such thing as one chocolate bar! Chocolate is dead to you now!

Learn to find a quiet place and breathe deeply. Sometimes it's our panic that drains us.

Improve your time spent at work by considering your needs deeply and making notes about your non-negotiables, before making future career decisions. Don't be afraid to be very specific, when journaling to gain clarity about your dream job.

Make a frequent practice of checking with yourself to see what has pulled you out of the vibrant stream of well-being and positive expectation.

Take time to walk in nature, allowing the high vibrations of the earth, the trees, the sun and wind, to cleanse, refresh and renew you. Walk by the sea whenever you can and allow the sparkles to caress your skin and soothe your jangled nerves.

Cleansing Negative Energies

Good hygiene is recognized as an excellent way to maintain health and prevent disease. The same principle that applies to hand washing holds true for subtle energetic cleansing as well. When the system is functioning well, energy is used efficiently, and there is neither a deficit nor excess. The vast majority of people are operating on a fraction of the energy available to the human system.

Proper focus and discipline are necessary in order to tap into — and efficiently use — these energy reserves. One of the steps in doing so is making sure you are not being bogged down with excess energy. This is something that tends to happen to empaths, and the accumulation sparks a myriad of issues. Anxiety, panic attacks, depression, lethargy, and other health problems are all possible if extra, negative energy is not cleansed from the system.

Thankfully, there are multiple ways to clear your aura. If you're feeling heavy, burdened, or if being bombarded by external sources has been a problem, it is a good idea to clear on a weekly or even daily basis. In time, it will be easier to know when clearing is necessary. A simple method is through prayer or use of a mantra. Many faiths have specific prayers or figures to call upon for protection, and this is an excellent way to accomplish your goal.

If this is not familiar, you can create a simple prayer asking that negative energy be removed from the system. Sacred sounds or "mantras" are recited to invoke what is being called upon. A Sanskrit mantra for protection of the body from oncoming danger is: "Om Hreem Hreem Hreem Hreem Hreem Hum Fatt". Chant this whenever you sense danger is coming towards you.

Smudging is another wonderful tool that has been around for ages. This is the burning of specific dried plants or resins whose smoke cleanses and drives away negative energy. Sage is the most well-known, but there are many different smudges including cedar, sweetgrass, lavender, mugwort, juniper, pinon, copal, frankincense, and myrrh. They have different properties, and can be combined for specific purposes. For example, sage is very good at cleansing, while sweetgrass is known to welcome positive energies.

Burning them together can be especially good. Smudge is either tied into a bundle called a "smudge stick" or comes loose and is burned in a fireproof vessel. Smudging is simple. Just light the smudge, blow out the flame, and pass or fan the smoke over the whole body. After the individual is smudged, smudge the room, home, or area as well — to remove any lurking, stagnant energy. This is another good practice to do regularly.

A bath with sea salt or sage clears the aura in a similar fashion. Sage baths have traditionally been used for sore and aching muscles, but are also beneficial for cleansing. To prepare a sage bath, do the following:

Take three ounces/100 grams of dried rubbing sage and put it in cheesecloth, a cotton pillowcase, or a knee-high stocking.

Tie off the end and place it into a bathtub full of hot water, like a tea bag. Let the bag of sage become wet, wring it out, and repeat a few times.

Remove the bag and soak in the waters for twenty minutes or more. The bag can be dried and reused up to three times.

Gemstones can act as an alternative, as they are also capable of cleansing negative energy. Fluorite is especially beneficial for removing bad energy from the aura, while amethyst and quartz balance and protect it. Placing a piece of selenite in each corner of the home after smudging can also be beneficial, as this creates a protective forcefield.

Amulets like a cross, yantra, or medicine wheel can be worn to ward off negative vibrations. Other tools like the mezuzah and hamsa hand can be used in the home to help maintain a positive energetic level.

Arts like feng shui are specifically designed to create harmony in one's living space. Empaths often feel like their home is their sanctuary and fortress against the world, but this can still be flooded by negative input. Deliberate arrangement and balance of the home optimizes how energy flows, and creates a rejuvenating place of rest.

If the negativity is triggering anxiety attacks, there are several simple, holistic steps you can take to help reverse the condition. They will be beneficial not only for panic attacks, but for any of the other symptoms as well.

1. Get deep, long-lasting sleep.

Too many people neglect their sleep, especially now that technology provides 24/7 entertainment. Keep your cell phone and any other unnecessary technology out of the bedroom. Making good quality sleep a priority will work wonders for agitation. Having a set bedtime helps establish a rhythm that tells the body it's time to rest. Avoiding overstimulation thirty minutes before hitting the sack is ideal and doing anything that helps one unwind, like reading, journaling, or meditating, sets the tone for a restful night. Scents like lavender promote relaxation and rest, as well as chamomile tea and natural sleep supplements like valerian root.

2. Eat well and exercise daily.

There are many, many diets and exercise programs out there, so keep it simple. Eat more fresh, wholesome foods with plenty of fruits and vegetables, and reduce or eliminate processed foods. Daily exercise can be as basic as starting the day with a ten minute walk or stretching. More vigorous daily activity works wonders for some, and mind-body exercises like yoga and tai chi are especially helpful for empaths. Their movements are designed to balance and harmonize the body's energy on a subtle level, while also strengthening the physical body.

3. Do breathing exercises.

The breath becomes quick and ragged when under stress. The quality of the breath is a direct gauge of one's emotions and state of mind. Take some time to observe your breath and see how often it is unsteady. Simple breathing exercises will quickly calm the mind, and help the body to relax and re-center. The following practice focuses on making the inhales and exhales of the same duration: Choose a count (four or six is good to start) and count to that number on the inhale. Exhale to the same count. Do this for a few minutes, or until the anxiety passes.

4. Avoid caffeine and other stimulants.

Stimulants may help with focus in the short term, but make anxiety skyrocket in the long term. This includes coffee, tea and, yes, even chocolate. Furthermore, stimulants are hard on the adrenal glands, the anatomy responsible for the fight-or-flight response and buffering stress. Good adrenal health is linked to a healthy root chakra. Try switching to decaf, herbal tea, or lemon water.

5. Mindfulness meditation.

The mind spends most of its time dwelling in the past or fretting over the future. Being mindful, or present in the now, is a panacea for the meandering and a cure for discontent. Mindfulness meditation can be performed when sitting quietly with crossed legs or in a straight-backed chair.

It really is as simple as it sounds:

a) As you are sitting, focus on the current setting.

b) Become aware of the sound of your breath, any other noises in the room, any smells or visuals.

c) Feel the cushion or chair under your body.

d) Any thoughts that arise in your mind are to be acknowledged and allowed to pass.

Doing this for ten or twenty minutes daily is recommended. It can also be done during any daily activities with the goal of being mindful in all tasks. When washing the dishes, for example, be present in the action. Do it slowly and lovingly. Be aware of every second of the action.

Mindfulness improves focus and reduces anxiety. It also makes people proactive instead of reactive. If an empath is being hit by a wave of input, mindful meditation will make it easier to think on one's feet and do what needs to be done to solve the situation rather than panicking and making it worse.

If an anxiety attack hits, grounding is the first step to take. Empaths can potentially receive waves upon waves of anxiety, and anchoring the system protects against external input. If this is ineffective, try mentally saying, "No!" with intent. It doesn't matter if you know where the waves are coming from or not. Refusing to allow the exchange can stop it dead in its tracks. Bending over and letting blood rush to the head will help with the spacey sensation, and tugging on the earlobes pacifies the system.

If you are at home or trying to sleep, wrapping blankets tightly around the body like a cocoon soothes and calms. Using any of the previously mentioned tools are an option, and sometimes all that is necessary is making contact with a close or loved one. If nothing is working, let the panic attack end naturally. Acknowledge that it is only anxiety and cannot cause any serious damage. Say that it will pass in five to fifteen minutes if one refuses to panic.

Do anything to make yourself more comfortable and then wait. Remember that prevention is the best cure, and experiment with ways to do away with the episodes.

Humans are a part of the natural world, but it is easy to forget this as we walk around in our concrete jungles. Experts warned the public at the turn of the century that big city-living is detrimental to health. Spending time in nature is one of the simplest and most effective ways to rebalance the system, ground, and rid the body of stagnant energy. It is especially important if you are currently residing in an urban area. Doing this regularly is a wonderful boost to health and happiness, and a potent preventative against falling ill.

Make spending time outdoors a regular part of your routine, and use this time as a source of pleasure. Bringing plants into your home and planting a garden are alternative or additional routes to take. Performing the aforementioned exercises in the wilderness can amplify their impact.

A more delicate matter is the healing of old emotional wounds. While the gifts of the empath are not pathological, many of the accompanying attitudes are. Poor boundaries, codependence, and being overly sensitive are signs of self-neglect. The empath who uses every technique available will only receive fleeting relief if old, underlying issues are not addressed.

They will be different depending on the person, and being brave enough to face these problems will be freeing in the long term. This kind of healing takes time and work, and may require a variety of interventions. Alternative medicine, energy healing, and bodywork will realign your physical energies and assist with removing that which hurts. Psychotherapy is another option, and others find release in solitude, contemplation, and self-reflection.

The power of love should never be underestimated, and tender relationships can be highly transformational in nature. Devotion and surrender to the bigger picture can instantly heal pain that no other efforts have been able to touch.

Stepping into a Deeper Purpose:

As soon as you have learned to prioritize your own wellbeing and have sorted out your emotional needs, you can discover the deeper spiritual purpose that you're meant for.

You have this ability for a reason.

Expressing in an Empowering way:

Simply suffering with someone doesn't do much to help them.

Rather than being a spectator to others' suffering, you can learn to express your empathy in ways that heal and empower others.

This empowering and healing can take many different forms, such as being a counselor or sharing powerful artwork.

You may find ways to integrate your empath nature into every social interaction you have.

For instance, as a parent, this skill would come in handy for communicating with your children. As a teacher, you could sense what is holding your student back and help them find the help they need.

The ability to connect using emotions can bring spiritual depth and true authenticity to your existence, helping others along the way.

Pay Close Attention to the Throat Chakra:

At times, the empath will be aware of exactly what they must do or say to create healthy boundaries, but then hesitate on expressing their need.

Our throat chakra is responsible for expressing personal truths, both verbal and otherwise.

When we intentionally clear any blockages in the throat chakra, we are opening ourselves up to the ability to share our truest feelings and needs.

Here are some methods for making sure your throat chakra stays open, healthy, and balanced.

Chanting or Singing: Since the throat chakra is tied to speech and expression, these are the quickest ways to open it up and free any blockages in the area.

Sharing your Thoughts: Although it can be a challenge, especially for the sensitive empath, sharing your feelings and ideas with people will help you unblock your throat chakra.

Pay Close Attention to your Root Chakra:

Another important chakra for empath balance is the root, which allows you to feel present in the physical world.

This enables you to feel grounded no matter what challenges pop up in your life.

Focusing more on this area will help you remain strong in yourself even when your emotions are going wild.

Here are some other useful tips for connecting with your root chakra.

Spending Time in Nature: As an empath, you likely already love to do this, but it helps immensely with grounding you in the physical world to make time to be outside.

Make sure you do this at least once a day, no matter what the weather is like.

Meditating on the Root Chakra: Simply thinking about and meditating on the root chakra can help you bring it into much-needed balance.

Conclusion

Being sensitive or empathic is something with which quite a few people are blessed. Sadly, the world is not understanding the importance of empathy.

Nowadays, no one seems to be happy. Don't our hearts bleed when we see our near and dear ones in pain? Don't we feel like extending our hand, pulling them into a hug and tell them that everything will be fine? These things are instinctive. They are physical and present. They are going on this moment and you can feel it in your bones. Yet it equally tough to find someone to lean upon when the world is slowly becoming desensitized to the emotions. Feeling sympathy is common, while empathetic gestures are increasingly becoming uncommon.

I am convinced that if each and every empath on our planet learnt more about how to harness this special gift and bring it out, then the world we live in would look very different. We are needed here and have great work to do, with that comes a great responsibility and we can only take this on by first taking care of ourselves. Once we know how to do this, only then can we extend and reach out to help others on their journey.

It is important to remember that everyone's experience of life is different. So, it is important you begin to look within yourself for more answers and recognize that the keys to change begin with you. Look at your life as a fun journey of self-exploration. If someone were to ask me now, if I would change my empathic nature, the simple answer would be no. I have learnt to work with and embrace all the gifts it has given me, without this ability I wouldn't be me.

I hope by using the knowledge in this book you're able to find more joy and fulfillment in your daily life. Everyone deserves to be happy but for some of us this can be more challenging. Stepping into your power and making a commitment to improve your life, is the single most important thing in creating change. So, look within for your courage. If there is one thing I have learnt from being an empath, that is that we are incredibly strong and can endure a lot. It is about time we started to direct this strength towards creating a happier and more joyful life for ourselves.

Once you learn to work with this gift, you will experience more incredible moments than you have ever known. A fully engaged empath, who knows how to manage their gift, can be so fully absorbed in reality that every moment becomes pure joy. Reaching this level takes dedication and work but with practice you'll experience the bliss of living a full life. Feeling every moment is the key to real joy and happiness.

Manufactured by Amazon.ca
Bolton, ON